The Best Homemade Food for Puppies

Nutritional Guide & Recipes for Raw & Cooked. FEDIAF & AAFCO Balanced.

Anne Benson, Dr. A Johnson

Ridgehill Publishing

Disclaimer

Nothing contained in this book is or should be considered or used as a substitute for veterinary medical advice, diagnosis, or treatment. The information provided in this book is for educational and informational purposes only and is not meant as a substitute for professional advice from a veterinarian or other professional.

This book and its contents do not constitute the practice of any veterinary medical or other professional veterinary health care advice, diagnosis, or treatment. The publishers and authors disclaim liability for any damages or losses, direct or indirect, that may result from the use of or reliance on information contained within the book.

Consumers are recommended to always seek the advice of a veterinarian, veterinary specialist, or other qualified veterinary health care provider with any questions regarding a pet's health or medical conditions. Never disregard, avoid, or delay in obtaining medical advice from your veterinarian or other qualified veterinary health care provider because of something you have read in this book. If you suspect your pet has a medical problem or condition, please immediately contact a qualified veterinary healthcare professional.

Free personalized recipe

Tailored specifically for your puppy

We would like to create a tailored recipe for you. To obtain this, please visit www.ridgehilldogs.com/free-recipe and submit your details. You will be sent a form to complete, providing us with details of your puppy, ingredient preferences, and anything else you wish us to consider. In line with your submission, we will create your recipe, which will be emailed to you.

We recommend you try a range of recipes in this book first to see your puppy's preferences and how readily you can obtain different ingredients. This will help you submit the best information and receive a recipe you will enjoy making, and your pup will enjoy eating!

Contents

Dedication

To Dr. Elizabeth Sampson

You have been with us since our dog breeding journey began, and we appreciate your help and practical assistance every step of the way. Your dedication to improving the health of Dalmatians has been inspirational, and you were our first introduction to fresh food feeding. Thank you for everything so far and all that is undoubtedly yet to come!

Acknowledgements

To all our wonderful puppy owners

Thank you for asking us so many questions about nutrition, which has prompted the research and writing of this book.

Foreword

Dr. Harry Street MRCVS

As Anne's uncle, I have known her for all her life. For as long as I can remember, Anne has been obsessed with animals! As a child, she collected pets like other little girls might collect dolls, and the pets only got bigger and more numerous as she grew up. From rare breed sheep to show goats and from beekeeping to fancy fowl, you never knew what would turn up next. It has been a particular delight to watch Anne enjoying Dalmatian breeding. She found her forte getting involved in improving the breed's genetics and fixing the long-standing uric acid problem that all of us vets dread when we see a Dalmatian walk into surgery.

This book is a great credit to you, Anne. Puppy nutrition is a modern minefield, and you have tackled the issue with your tenacity for research yet made it reader-friendly for owners. I am also grateful to see those low-purine recipes for Dalmatians. Well done.

Nutritional Guide

For Healthy Puppies

The frightening truth: "A study at the University of California, Davis School of Veterinary Medicine, analyzed 200 different recipes for home-prepared dog food recipes.....from websites, veterinary textbooks, and pet care books. The findings highlighted that 95% of the recipes were deficient in at least one essential nutrient and 84% were lacking in multiple required nutrients."[2]

For lifelong dog health, it is vitally important that puppies are fed correctly during their formative growth period. You only get one chance to get it right, and puppy nutrition is critically different from that of adult dogs [1,4]. The recipes in this book have been written by **Anne Benson, renowned breeder,** and **health screening advocate, with the support of vet Dr. Alex Johnson MRCVS,** following the most up-to-date scientific research and current formulation guidelines.

Creating homemade puppy food is a rewarding endeavor that offers numerous health benefits for your beloved canine companion but is not to be taken lightly. We fear for the health of a generation of puppies growing up on simple internet diets, which are vastly lacking in critically essential nutrients and contain excesses that can be equally damaging.

Puppies fed an inappropriate or unbalanced diet have an increased risk of a wide range of very real problems being seen in vet surgeries across the country and indeed globally, including behavioral and mood disorders such as **anxiety & aggression** [3,15], **compromised immune system** leading to a reduced immune response to vaccines and infections[4] **spinal curvatures, stunted growth, fractured growth plates, early hip dysplasia, and other musculoskeletal problems** [4,5,7,11,19,21,22,23] problems with cognitive development and **reduced trainability** [9,13] **coat problems**[10,18], **autoimmune disorders**[4], **liver disease** [16], **predisposition to obesity & diabetes** as adult dogs [1,4,5] and a myriad of other issues. You can read all the research links in the resources section of this book for a sad collection of scientific evidence or simply ask an experienced vet.

Many of these problems could have been avoided with correct puppy nutrition. It is tragically sad to see the results of deficiency, poor advice, excesses, and incorrect mineral, vitamin, and nutrient ratios during the critical puppyhood foundation and growth phases.

Correctly balanced full-spectrum puppy nutrition is laying a foundation for lifelong health. It's not just about whipping up a batch of goodies; it's about taking control of your puppy's nutrition and giving them the best start in a long, energy-filled, healthy life. In an era where health awareness is paramount, many health-conscious owners take the initiative to ensure their pets eat with as much emphasis on health and well-being as they do themselves.

This book aims to help you deliver all these amazing benefits and avoid poor nutrition's terrible consequences and pitfalls. **We are giving you the tools, information, and recipes** you need to create homemade meals that are:

- Fresh and wholesome

- Perfectly balanced according to growth stage, age, and breed

- Packed with superfoods that offer specific health benefits

- Tailored to any food sensitivities or genetic predispositions

- Tailored for optimum growth rate - neither too rapid nor too slow

Science shows us that the correct puppy nutrition can:

- Improve their intelligence and trainability

- Improve their immune response to both vaccines and infections

- Ensure optimal musculoskeletal development

- Improve their mental health and behavior as adults

- Reduce the risk of a wide range of chronic diseases in later life

- Reduce the likelihood of adult obesity, diabetes, and connected health problems

- Reduce the likelihood of hormone disorders

- Reduce the likelihood of autoimmune disorders

- Extend their health closer to end of life

- Extend their actual lifespan

- And more

"The goal of a feeding plan for puppies is to create a healthy adult. The specific objectives of a good puppy feeding plan are to achieve healthy growth, optimize trainability and immune function, and minimize obesity and developmental orthopedic disease....nutrition has proved to be the most important non-genetic factor for healthy bone development"[4]

Having the power to control every ingredient in your pet's bowl can be a game-changer. Homemade puppy food is a proactive approach to managing your puppy's health, not just now but for life. It allows ingredient control, nutritional enhancement with superfoods, and support for a healthy microbiome. It's a labor of love that results in complete, balanced, tasty meals and a healthier, happier dog that can enjoy life with you to the fullest.

Understanding nutrients in puppy health and growth

Macro and micro-nutrients

Macro-nutrients. These are proteins, carbohydrates, and fats.

Proteins. Let's start by looking at protein. Puppy meals should contain sufficient protein to support healthy growth.[1,4] Excess protein has not been scientifically shown to have any negative impact on their growth, but insufficient protein stunts growth [5]

Variable protein sources such as a wide range of meat, offal, and fish not only provide the full range of essential amino acids (the building blocks for new tissue growth) but also carry all sorts of other micronutrients, which we will come to later. Generally speaking, for the vast majority of breeds, the more variable their protein sources, the better.

An occasional challenge in this regard can be dogs with genetic problems that prevent such variety. Ask your vet if your chosen breed has any metabolism problems with specific nutrients. For example, most Dalmatians must have low-purine diets. As Nua(Lua) Dalmatian breeders, we are sadly only too aware that not all breeders understand or are transparent about such issues, so please check with your vet and get your puppy tested if recommended.

Fats in your puppy's diet provide energy density and important micronutrients. Certain vitamins are fat soluble, so fats are vital, but the correct types must be balanced to provide the full range of nutrients and the correct ratio with each other. A more common problem with fat is simply feeding too much. If a puppy gets fat, it produces more fat cells. If an adult dog gets fat, it stretches the fat cells it already has but does not create more. This is important, as an adult dog with more fat tissue gets fat more easily. It is vitally important that puppies don't get overweight as this will create more fat tissue and therefore predispose them to obesity when adults. Dog obesity, much like us humans, is a hugely growing problem and brings with it all the same life-shortening and sickness problems that we hear of regularly - cardiac issues, diabetes, immune problems, joint problems, shortened lifespan, and more. We choose how much to eat, but our puppies and dogs have their calories controlled by us. We, as owners, are, therefore, entirely responsible for our dog's weight and body condition. To feed your puppy to fatness is cruelty, not kindness.

Carbohydrates (ideally only 5-15% of the bowl) are commonly thought of as energy-providing, which is true, but they can be so much more. In commercial food, bulking agents are often high-energy, low-value carbs like refined grains and flours. We have so many better options. Our recipes provide complex carbs of a wide range, including all sorts of additional nutrients and important fibre. Different carbohydrate sources have been show to have a beneficial effect on the microbiome. This is why we stick to these complex healthy ingredients, such as vegetables and pulses.

Nuts and Seeds - where do we put these? Proteins? Fats? Carbs? They overlap all these categories but can tend to be fat-heavy. They harbor a fantastic range of different micronutrients not easily found in other ingredients, so you will find them in many recipes but generally in small quantities to try and keep that fat balance in control.

Fiber. Considered essential in humans for a healthy bowel, the purpose of fiber in puppies is rather different. We have a very long and relatively slow gut, so fiber helps keep our insides clean and moving. It can take several days for our food to pass right through, but dogs have a much shorter gut. What you feed in the morning, you might see coming through in the afternoon and evening or certainly by the next day. So their need for fiber is reduced, but it has been shown to improve their microbiome when in the form of complex mixed ingredients like pulses. Fibre can help with satiety in dogs with big appetites, which helps control weight, but this is really an issue more associated with adult dogs.

Micronutrients. These are our vitamins, minerals, and trace elements.

A lack or an excess of vitamins or minerals can have perhaps the most devastating impact on your puppy's health, present and future. These elements are most difficult to estimate and often missing in simple internet diets. Analyzed figures must be used to provide the best estimates of foods' and ingredients' vitamin and mineral content to balance your puppy's diet safely. Balance is everything for your growing pup.

Beneficial bacteria

The puppy microbiome is a relatively new area of research. Most of us have gained awareness of the human microbiome, and so we appreciate its importance, but research specific to puppies and dogs is growing all the time. The microbiome can be viewed as part of your puppy's immune system just as much as being part of its digestive system.

So, we have covered what the different nutritional elements provide for a growing puppy, but what happens if we get it wrong? Let's dive into the science-backed specifics.

Balance and imbalance results for puppies

- both short and long term implications

You can have too much and too little of a good thing. This section is to inform but not to worry you - it is not good reading for the faint of heart! This is not an exhaustive list but highlights some of the better-known and researched issues associated with a lack of, or excess of, something in your puppy's diet. By being informed, you can make the best choices. As more research comes to light, the necessity for the correct balance of these nutrients is ever more apparent. It is also important to appreciate that your puppy's needs change throughout its growth period, so our recipe formulations vary by growth stage.[25] There are recipes for puppies under 50% of their anticipated adult weight, from 50 to 80%, and from 80 to 100% of adult weight. We will show you how to know when your puppy has moved to the next growth phase.

All our recipes are balanced and meet the requirements for optimal growth, health, and longevity, so if you prefer not to read this section, which quite frankly can be sad, then feel free to skip it with confidence. You don't necessarily need to know what you are avoiding, but we know that for some readers, it is important to fully understand exactly why it is worth making the effort to feed a full-spectrum balanced diet.

Proteins.

As mentioned, insufficient protein will stunt growth as it provides amino acids - the building blocks for new tissue. 11 essential amino acids must be provided in your puppy's diet. Others are important for health but can be synthesized by your puppy from these 11, provided they have all the other correct nutrients to support the process. [43]

A lack of some essential amino acids has been shown to be responsible for behavioral issues such as anxiety and aggression. Arginine, glycine, methionine, serine, taurine, tryptophan, and tyrosine are important in this regard, but especially notable is tryptophan. Liver and certain seeds are particularly good sources, but large quantities are not required - balance is required in everything. [3] Proteins found in mushrooms have also been shown to improve immune response, and general protein deficiency is a frequent cause of secondary immunodeficiency. [5]

Tryptophan deficiency is particularly associated with greater and uncontrolled aggression, so we don't want our puppies to lack this important nutrient to develop into mentally well-balanced adults. If dogs are required for controlled aggressive roles, this is achieved via training and would never be improved by nutrient deficiency, just in case some readers might be raising protection dogs. [15]

The **Lysine** discussion. There is an amino acid called Lysine around which some controversy exists over safe levels. One (FEDIAF), but not others (AAFCO & NRC), of the regulatory bodies for animal feed specification and legislation recommend a maximum limit for this amino acid when it is added to processed puppy food in a purified, isolated form. [25, 26, 27, 28] This particular amino acid varies greatly in its bioavailability depending on both the source and how it is processed. Deficiency stunts growth, but a study also showed that an excess can stunt growth by interfering with arginine metabolism in a purified additive form. [40] The studies in this area are new, ongoing, and aimed at the commercial feed industry, so at the moment, they are focused on purified forms used as additives. They also state that additional research is required as... "the mechanism behind the lysine-arginine antagonism in the dog remains to be elucidated (explained)." [38,39,40]

Having interviewed vets on the matter, the consensus seems that higher levels of Lysine in its natural form within whole foods are not known to produce negative effects. Vets who specialize in nutritional formulation for puppies do not consider or take account of any maximum level for this, provided it is not added in an artificially purified supplement form. Keeping this amino acid below the levels suggested for manufacturers of processed foods would lead to problematic restrictions on other nutrients when formulating a wholefood-based diet as it is an abundant amino acid found in many if not most, protein sources. As with many nutrients within whole foods, alongside other compounds, puppies may metabolize or utilize them in ways not yet understood. In formulating, we have not allowed this threshold to restrict the range and variety of protein sources beneficial for balancing a wide range of micronutrients. N.B. Don't forget that 2 of the main global regulatory bodies don't even have a suggested threshold. Still, as we consider all research and all recommendations, it felt important to make readers aware of them.

Carbs. People talk of carbs being essential for energy, but dogs are not people. Most of a puppy's energy requirements will be met from fats, and due to differences in their metabolism compared to people, they do not suffer a lack of energy with low carbohydrate intake. [41] This doesn't mean we must avoid all carbs, but they do not play a large nutritional role, provided the diet is balanced in other respects.

When making homemade puppy feed, we do not need "fillers," which is the most common use of carbs in commercial formulations. We mainly gain carbs in these recipes through complex whole foods, which provide many micronutrients to balance the diet. Sweet potatoes and pulses, such as chickpeas & lentils, have been shown to improve digestion and moderate blood sugar levels[6]. We want to introduce them, but a word of caution: Under 12 weeks of age, puppies cannot effectively digest starch. It can ferment in the gut and cause diarrhea, interfering with other nutrient absorption. So complex carbs are best introduced gradually and in small quantities from 12 weeks on. [5] We, therefore, restrict starchy carbs in the earliest growth stage recipes.

You may well notice some recipes with no obvious carbs, and yet their nutritional profile will show carbs. Look again, and you will likely find fresh vegetables, fruit, nuts, and seeds but perhaps none of the obvious grains and heavily starchy veg as they can unbalance recipes by reducing the % of healthy fats and necessary proteins. Don't feel you need to see rice, potatoes or beans in a recipe for your puppy to have enough energy, simply not true! They will feature here and there for variety but only in a fully balanced recipe, so their percentage will be small.

Fats, fats, and more fats.

I know I risk repeating myself, but you must ensure your puppy does not get fat. You can have too much of a good thing. Healthy fats are exactly that, but only in moderation, such as provided in these balanced recipes. Obesity in adult dogs can start in puppyhood, and just like humans, it is becoming the biggest causal factor in disease and early death. Total fat percentage, whilst relatively high for puppy energy requirements, must not get out of hand.

Fats come in 3 basic forms:

Saturated - too much can harden cell walls

Monounsaturated - improves flexibility of cell walls

Polyunsaturated - these can be short or long chain.

All broken fats release fatty acids, the important nutritional factors.

Adult dogs can create most of the fatty acids they require from a single type, linoleic acid, but puppies lack the correct enzymes to do this. Therefore, in puppy diets, there are 8 essential fatty acids that must be provided via differing fat sources. These essential fatty acids are crucial in numerous physiological processes, including cardiovascular development and brain function. They have anti-inflammatory properties and improve immune system development, eyesight & hearing development, behavioral attitude, and trainability.[4,5,7,53]

These are the essential fatty acids for puppies that we balance in our recipes:

1. LA linoleic acid

2. ALA alpha–linolenic acid

3. AA - arachidonic acid

4. EPA eicosapentaenoic acid

5. DPA Docosapentaenoic acid

6. DHA docosahexaenoic acid

7. Omega 6

8. Omega 3

We also balance the important ratio between Omega 6 & 3 and ensure the total combination of EPA and DHA does not exceed the recommended healthy maximum.

Vitamins

Vitamins are important in so many biological processes. Many of us will recall well-known examples from human historical discoveries, such as Vitamin C from citrus fruits resolving the mysterious scurvy disease of sailors. To list all vitamin deficiency problems here would be to cover almost every metabolic and growth process known. Needless to say, a wide range of vitamins in the correct proportions is essential. Some of the most commonly studied for puppies and that we ensure are balanced in our recipes include A, C, D, E, B1, B2, B3, B5, B6, B12, Folic acid (B9), Choline, K1 and Biotin (B7).

In brief, these are some of the effects seen if puppies are deficient in any of these vitamins but remember this is not intended to frighten, merely to inform. With the understanding you are armed and with balanced diets, we should be able to avoid them altogether:

Vitamin A - skeletal changes and nervous system problems.[44]

Vitamin C - scurvy has wide-ranging problems, including immunity issues, anemia, skeletal problems, and more, but it's rarely seen in puppies these days.

Vitamin D deficiency will affect bone development in a similar way to rickets in humans, but an excess of vitamin D can lead to intoxication and even death in the worst-case scenario. [5]

Vitamin E - is important for the immune system and inflammation [45]

Water soluble B vitamins are important for neurological development [9]

Folic acid (B9) & Niacin (B3) work together. Deficiency can produce growth and anemia problems, even leading to death. [46]

Choline - In a compilation of research studies, "Diets are described on which fatal deficiency of choline in weanling puppies, accompanied by severe fatty infiltration of the liver, could be induced in less than 3 weeks." The reasons and what happens in the body are quite complex. There is also some contention in the research. Puppies can make choline themselves from other nutrients, although perhaps not sufficiently to meet their needs, the levels specified by the regulatory bodies seem to be based on older and small-scale studies. We can only work with what we have, so while we watch for more research on the topic, we have formulated choline levels that meet the guidelines. [25, 47,48]

K1 - Important in the process of blood coagulation and bone mineralization. [49]

Biotin (B7) - This is another nutrient that your puppy can synthesize in their intestines with a healthy microflora, but not necessarily at the levels required for growth. There is some research around egg white binding biotin, making it unavailable, but the studies were on animals fed egg white as a sole source of protein. If our puppies have the equivalent of a single raw egg, this is not seen to cause an issue, but if you have problems with other protein sources and choose to feed a lot of eggs, then it may be worth cooking the whites, eliminating this problem. In recipes that contain more than 10% egg, we remind you to consider cooking the whites to avoid any potential biotin absorption issues.

Minerals, including trace elements. Can we say one is more important than another? Well, maybe not so simply, but of all the mineral imbalances that affect puppies and their growth, Calcium, and Phosphorus are right up there at the top of the chart.

Sufficient calcium is absolutely vital for the rapid bone growth occurring during puppyhood, but it must be in the correct proportion to **phosphorus** for that growth to be healthy. **Vitamin D** is also required for these 2 minerals to be used by the body in laying down healthy bones. If you remember nothing else from this section, please take this to heart - **do not supplement any of these recipes with additional calcium**. This is one of the single most common mistakes a puppy owner can make by thinking that more calcium will lead to stronger bones. Calcium deficiency is important to avoid, but it is rare these days, with more puppies having problems from an excess or incorrect Ca:P ratio rather than insufficient. [5, 7, 21, 23, 28, 29] Sadly many of us, breeders and vets across the country, regularly see avoidable Ca:P related deformities and problems.

Again, we could examine a myriad of possible symptoms for other mineral deficiencies and excesses, but let's focus on those most well recognised and measured in research. In our formulations, in addition to Calcium and Phosphorus, we balance Potassium, Sodium, Magnesium, Chloride, Iron, Copper, Manganese, Zinc, Iodine, and Selenium, so let's briefly examine these.

Potassium - Deficiency results in low growth rates, changes in cardiac rhythms, and, tragically, within 3 to 8 weeks, paralysis of the legs. [50] I have also witnessed this paralysis in a pair of twins born to a deficient mother. It was considered irreversible, but with huge amounts of care along with injections and other supplements, the twins eventually walked and even ran but could never be considered fully 'normal' in their physical gait. Potassium also operates with sodium, as explained next.

Sodium—Dogs are approximately 60% water. About 2/3rds of this water is inside cells, and ⅓ is outside cells. In relatively simple terms, this ratio is important and is maintained by biological pumps in cell membranes operated by sodium and potassium. The correct operation ensures correct fluid pressures in the right places for optimal movement of other substances. This impacts virtually all body systems, although the circulatory and nervous systems are often affected the most.

Magnesium Deficiency leads to lowered weight gain, hyperirritability, convulsions, and changes in blood vessels and heart muscle tissue.

Chloride deficiency - Failure to thrive and stunted forelimb growth.[51] Although rare I have seen this in kittens. If diagnosed early enough growth can be caught up via supplementation and forelimb growth may catch up but I was unable to follow up the kittens long term so I have no knowledge of their adult outcome.

Iron - Probably the most well-known issue with iron deficiency is anemia leading to fatigue and retarded growth. Anemia also exacerbates anemia. Red blood cells weakened by inadequate iron are fragile and short-lived, leading to greater anemia and a vicious cycle. There are also more hidden problems associated with iron deficiency. It impairs the operation of the small intestine and, therefore, the absorption of nutrients. This, in turn, can lead to a deficiency of other nutrients that cannot be absorbed due to this problem. So iron deficiency can show itself in a wide range of symptoms, but all will present with anemia, which gives vets the biggest clue as to what may be causing other symptoms. There are so many interesting aspects of how a puppy manages iron, but I must remember that this is not a vet manual! To learn more, visit the resource articles and follow their references to read the articles they cite. Excess iron is generally not an issue as the body prevents it from being absorbed above a safe level. [54,55]

Copper. Deficiency can lead to coat color abnormalities, muscle weakness, and unseen bone problems, which may present in later life. Copper excess can lead to toxicity, resulting in liver disease, but this is rare without a genetic predisposition for it. Such genetic predisposition, if suspected, can be tested for. It is more common in Bedlington Terriers [16]

Manganese is necessary for the action of many enzymes and, therefore, a range of biological processes. It is significant in the metabolism of carbs, protein, and cholesterol. A lack of Manganese leads to problems with bone formation, digestion, and general development. [56]

Zinc can help moderate copper storage and is important in a multitude of biological functions, including immunity, wound healing, and skin condition.[42] Almost all the published puppy food recipes we tested were zinc deficient.

Iodine - Many people associate iodine with thyroid problems, and this is the same for puppies. Excess iodine leads to hypothyroidism, leading to problems and changes in bone formation during growth. Inadequate iodine leads to hyperthyroidism, lethargy, and reduced growth. While the thyroid does an excellent job of regulating iodine, it is important to control dietary iodine within quite a tight range to optimize health.[57]

Selenium is an essential trace element with antioxidant properties. It is associated with thyroid hormone metabolism and the immune system. More recently, it has been discovered that selenium supports the gut microbiome, reduces intestinal inflammation, and improves the gut environment for healthy bacteria. [58]

Microbiome. The last decade has seen microbiome research expand rapidly as it has become apparent that it forms an integral part of animal immunity. The range of healthy organisms that live in puppies' guts helps to train their immune systems. In turn, their immune systems work to maintain a symbiotic, beneficial relationship with this microflora of the intestines. Antibiotics, which can be life-saving, can negatively impact the microbiome. In young puppies, the early months are particularly important in establishing the long-term intestinal flora, so if possible, try to avoid antibiotics but balance this with a sensible approach. If a puppy has an infection, it can deteriorate faster than you can imagine. Don't be deterred from utilizing antibiotics to potentially save their life, but avoid a "just in case" antibiotic policy when it is sensible to do so.

Look after the microbiome during any dietary transition. The biggest change for a young puppy is moving to their new home. Whatever they have been fed on, even if you feel it is unsuitable, don't change it too rapidly. Changing diet during this already stressful period without a transition phase can lead to diarrhea, a drastic change in the intestinal flora, and a resultant increased risk of bacterial or viral infection. This can initiate a vicious cycle of treatment, microbiome upset, and dietary changes to try and support recovery, and so it goes around. Take things slowly and add both probiotics and prebiotics to meals to support any period of change.

"The supplementation of puppy diet (8 weeks old) with probiotics induces a better specific immune response." Lactobacillus or Enterococcus faecium are suitable examples among others available on the market. Even very young puppies can benefit from pre and pro-biotics. We have supported 'failing' newborn puppies with probiotic treatments with remarkable success. [5,32,33,34,35,58]

For those of you who chose to read this section, I hope you have found it as fascinating as I do, but if not, do not despair! The important thought to take away is that these recipes are formulated for very specific reasons and are always in the best long-term interest of your puppy.

Differing standards

AAFCO, NRC, FEDIAF. [25,26,27]

So....who decides what a full spectrum balanced recipe is for a growing young puppy? There is a growing body of research (as seen in the preceding section) demonstrating what puppies need and must avoid to be healthy as they grow to adulthood, but who looks at all of this, pulls it together, and creates a meaningful reference standard? We can be as cynical about "the system" as we like, but we need something to work with, and we have to accept that no one knows everything and imperfection is everywhere, so let's be as sensible as possible.

There are currently 3 main regulatory/advisory bodies for the constituents of pet food manufacture. These are the:

- Association of American Food Control Officials

- FEDIAF - the trade body that represents the European pet food industry

- The National Research Council (NRC) oversees the National Animal Nutrition Program (NANP)

All of these focus on the pet food industry and controlling what goes into processed dog food, which is sold to the public in packets, tins, bags, etc. For the purposes of this book, we are concentrating on complete puppy food. 'Complete' foods when sold ought to contain the minimum requirements laid out in the specifications to be labeled as 'complete' or clearly show on the label that they are complementary and not 'complete'. Unfortunately, some online retailers are flouting this. We found plenty of examples of 80:10:10 mixes of meat, offal, and bone being labeled as "complete" without any suggestion of meeting the standards.

These bodies, while giving guidance levels for nutrients, are primarily focused on legal labeling of products for sale to the public. Of the 3, FEDIAF keeps the most up-to-date and adjusts its guidelines in line with fresh research each year—although it is still primarily funded by pet food manufacturers, so let's hope this does not bias which papers it considers.

These bodies must exist to reduce the problem of manufacturers selling anything vaguely viable as dog food and making claims without basis. So I am not knocking them....but.... There is always a "but," right? We can use their guidance to create better health for our puppies and dogs than processed food. What makes me think that? A certain amount of common sense and population evidence. Think of people you know who eat fresh, healthy, home-prepared food compared with those who primarily eat processed food. Generally, we see in the population that fresh food eaters are healthier than those eating predominantly processed food.

Puppies are not people, but it surely appeals to any common sense that if we can meet the nutritional guidelines with fresh whole foods and avoid intense processing, filling, purified extracted ingredients, and preservatives (that are required for long shelf life), surely our puppies will reflect this in their health and longevity. Studies and advisory bodies on homemade dog food recipes do not yet exist. They may come, but without an industry sponsoring them, they may not. So, instead, let us use the best of what is available by adhering to current guidelines, keeping up to date with research currently underway, and formulating fresh, balanced, whole-food recipes for our dogs.

When people come to ask for diet and recipe formulations, they will often request an AAFCO diet because that is the big name they hear. AAFCO is all about the pet food industry label standards. Because FEDIAF reviews research and updates its guidelines annually, we choose to formulate most of our recipes following FEDIAF standards. Still, we do some to AAFCO as some people want that. Each recipe will tell you which standard they comply with. The only difference we make regarding FEDIAF recipes is in Lysine content. As discussed in the protein section, we do not constrain the overall level of lysine as it is never added in purified supplemental form and is only provided in whole food from natural protein sources. This doesn't apply to AAFCO as they have no upper limit. All recipes show you the full nutrient profile, including micro-nutrients.

Puppy growth rates

The missing ingredient in long-term health

Puppy growth is not a race; new research shows it must be carefully controlled to ensure optimum adult health and longevity. We all hear of giant breeds, in particular, being affected by growth disorders, but labradors and dogs in the mid-size range are also very negatively affected by overly rapid growth. As experienced breeders, we discourage our new puppy owners from comparing straight lb or kg weights with their puppy's litter mates in our support groups. Instead, we focus on healthy growth rates. [5,29]

The healthiest growth rate for puppies is determined by breed and sex. Small dogs mature in as little as 12 months, medium dogs take 15 to 18 months and large breeds 2 years to complete their growth.

Puppies growing too slowly may have unlying health problems or malnutrition. Those that grow too fast risk health problems in later life. In particular, overly rapid growth can predispose to obesity as fat puppies actually create extra lifelong fat tissue. Fast growth in large breed dogs can be particularly damaging and is directly connected to skeletal problems. The greatest nutritional influence on the incidence of hip dysplasia occurs when energy is restricted very early in life. So, when you have made such an effort to seek out a conscientious breeder who screens, scores, and maintains tip-top joints in their breeding lines, let's bolster that further with the right nutritional foundation for their future joint health.[4,5,7,29]

Don't be overwhelmed. How do we get it right? It is not at all difficult, but like anything, you need a little bit of effort and practice in the first few weeks.

It is important to weigh your puppy regularly and compare their growth to benchmark charts for their breed and sex. You can download **free puppy growth rate charts** online at www.waltham.com/resources/puppy-growth-charts, where you will also find easy information and FAQs on how to use them. Here's a brief overview: [30,31]

Choose the correct chart for your puppy's gender and how heavy you expect them to be as adults. If you don't know this final anticipated weight, you can ask your breeder or your vet, look on the kennel club website for breed standard weights, or ask the breeder about parent weights if a crossbreed. If your puppy is a rescue puppy of entirely unknown parentage, your vet is the most likely person to be able to give you a guide. You do not need to know precisely, but it helps you choose which chart to start with.

Find your puppy's starting weight - the breeder should know how much they weighed at collection, and your most recent vet visit will have another weight. Plot these on the chart at the correct age points, along with today's weight. See which centile lines your puppy fits between and ask yourself (and your vet), "Is my puppy looking and feeling a healthy weight?" We will look at healthy weights and body condition scoring in a moment.

Each week, or 2 at the most, re-weigh your puppy and plot their weight on the chart. Throughout their growth period, they may cross a line into a different centile section on the chart, but crossing 2 lines is a red flag. For example, let's say your puppy started in between the 9th and 25th centile lines. As they grow, they may move into the 2 - 9 centile gap, or they may move into the 25 to 50 centile gap. In either case, they will have crossed 1 line but not 2 lines. If they moved over into another centile gap, this indicates their growth appears to be either too slow or too fast for optimum health.

Another vital skill to get started on from the beginning is Body Condition Scoring or BCS. When you download the growth charts at www.waltham.com/resources/puppy-growth-charts, search for Body Condition Scoring on that website, as they have a video discussing how to do it. Each day, get accustomed to looking at your puppy with a critical eye and asking yourself - do they have a defined waist tuck from the side and looking down from the top? Can you feel their ribs easily with your hands but not count them with your eyes? This is a health skill for life and will help you know, day by day if you are feeding enough or too much. BCS will also help you notice a growth spurt before it appears on your weekly chart. A puppy can rapidly grow and lose condition if their food allowance isn't increased accordingly, so as you only weigh and plot once a week or once a fortnight, you may see them jump down a line or even 2 on the charts, which could have been avoided with BCS as you would feel and see the change in their shape and ribs and adjust accordingly. Once learned, it is a life skill to keep your dog healthy. Don't fret over BCS, but keep practicing as you plot your puppy's growth chart, and you will soon gain confidence.

How much to feed? How can we calculate a starting point of how much to actually feed before all this weighing and BCS starts to become second nature? We need a baseline, right? Weigh your puppy and convert it into kg. This is their body weight BW. The approx. kcal they need each day is calculated from their current weight but always adjusts up or down according to BCS. Body condition is far more important and valuable to your puppy's health than a number in a book.

The math - (BW is the current puppy's body weight):

For puppies less than 50% of their expected adult weight:

- BW x 157.5 = kcals of food for 1 day

For puppies between 50% and 80% of expected adult weight:

- BW x 131.25 = kcals of food for 1 day

For puppies, 80% of adult weight to maturity

- BW x 105 = kcals of food for 1 day

Once mature, it will depend upon activity and living conditions:

- BW x 94 to 105 but constantly refined and determined by ongoing BCS.

These calculations give you an estimate of the daily amount of food in kcals. Every recipe gives you a kcal per 100g and per ounce, so you can easily weigh out meal portions. [4]

Your puppy's daily allowance should be divided into multiple meals, starting from 4 meals at 8 weeks old and gradually down to 2 meals at maturity.

At this point, we must talk about treats. Using the wrong treats and/or taking no notice of them could double your puppy's calcium intake and add significantly to their calories, so treats must be accounted for to ensure puppy health. In this book are some training treat recipes that are balanced the same way as meals so you can feed them without imbalance concerns, but you must still include their calorie count in the puppy's daily allowance. If you buy commercial treats, keep the small quantities and watch your body condition scoring. If threats creep up, you risk unbalancing important minerals.

Supplements & Substitutions

& Nutrient value problems of certain ingredients

If you see recipes on the internet or in books labeled as suitable for puppies but containing only half a dozen basic ingredients, I'm sorry, but it simply cannot be true. To obtain the full range of nutrients puppies need in their meals, a wide range of ingredients is required. You have already seen the extensive list of vitamins and minerals needed, and even superfoods don't hold all of these, hence the need for variety.

Some of the challenges

Certain nutrients can be challenging to get in the correct quantities or ratios in whole foods without always using the same ingredients. We have tried to ensure variety, but certain items you will see occur frequently, and occasionally, we will utilize good quality supplements of specific minerals. For example:

- Oysters are great for zinc. We sometimes use a zinc supplement to avoid putting oysters in virtually every recipe. With any mineral supplements, you must pay attention to the total mg in the recipe. So you can substitute for a locally available brand, but check the total mg of that mineral, e.g., zinc, in that particular brand of tablet or capsule and for that total recipe. Chelated minerals are generally best for bioavailability, so look for chelated zinc. (Avoid supplements that are sulfates or oxides of minerals.) In some recipes, if the exchange is simple enough, we have offered the zinc supplement replacement option for oysters.

- Beef liver is a fantastic source of copper, but again, it might not agree with some puppies or might not be available, and we don't want it in every recipe, so sometimes, we might again use a copper supplement. As for zinc, look for chelated versions and check for the total mg required in the recipe. Caution: dried liver is not as nutrient-rich as fresh, so again, try to get fresh to retain the balance of recipes.

- Spleen is fabulous for iron but simply not on the average grocery store shelf. So again, you may see us use a supplement to provide practical options for people who use different recipes.

- Kelp is pretty much our sole source of iodine, but you must check that the kelp powder you buy states the micrograms of iodine per gram of kelp, as kelps can vary significantly in their iodine content. If it doesn't, then buy another brand that does. We have formulated 700mcg of iodine per gram of kelp powder, so if you have a different one, do the math to match the number of grams required.

- Calcium & Phosphorous - We have the statistics to include these safely in whole food forms such as chicken wings, but this presents a different challenge. Not just that, you need a mincer! Chicken wings are high in fat, and we must ensure that our total fat content isn't too high. We need to include fat-soluble vitamins, which means having different fats, oils, seeds, or nuts in the recipes, and these together can easily tip us over into the higher ranges we are trying to avoid for total fat percentage. The specific levels of calcium and phosphorous in wings, necks, and backs will also have a range of natural variability. For these reasons, we often revert to using only bone meal in the earliest growth stage recipes as this gives us a measurable way to obtain our calcium and some of the needed phosphorous while not increasing fats. You will see more natural bone sources in other growth-stage recipes, but the final balance is still obtained via bonemeal. If we raise the percentage of bone in recipes much higher than 10% puppies can struggle with constipation but 10% rarely provides sufficient mineral content without supplementation.

- This fat problem is also an issue with meats, which is why you'll find that most of the main protein sources are lean meats. We need the fat allowance for other ingredients that bring important vitamins and minerals into the recipe, so don't swap 90:10% lean beef for 70:30%

If an ingredient is difficult to obtain in your area, first take a look at our suggested suppliers in Chapter 12. If this doesn't help, then try searching online. We cannot buy spleen locally, but we buy online and freeze. I buy beef liver when I see it in the store as it comes and goes and is often in the reduced-price section. Again, I'll simply freeze it for future use. Kidneys & hearts are the same. Offal has so very many valuable nutrients. You will see it in many, if not most, of the recipes. There is a theory that when wild canines bring down prey, they always eat the offal first, as it is nutrient-rich. The good news is the quantities required for a balanced recipe are relatively low compared to the overall recipe weight, so a little goes a long way. As offal is so nutrient-dense, it is important not to be 'generous' and add extra, or you may unwittingly exceed safe max levels for some minerals or vitamins.

Making friends with a local butcher, farmer, or game hunter can be valuable as they often have offal. We keep sheep, so we have plenty of lamb offal and tripe, which are not otherwise readily available. If they shoot in the nearby woods, we can often get organs meat-free by simply lending a hand as they clean and dress the deer in situ.

In conclusion, we appreciate that accessibility to certain ingredients, particularly offal and organ meat, can be a challenge. Ask around, visit local rural areas to contact farmers or hunters if you have any nearby, look online, ask in natural/raw feeding Facebook groups, or look for a different recipe (which is another reason we have tried to be as variable as possible).

Superfoods include foods high in antioxidants and unusually dense in a range of beneficial micronutrients. Such foods support healthy growth and a flourishing microbiome. Antioxidants increase immune response to vaccines and long-term immunity, so less frequent vaccinations are required.[5] For vegetables and fruit, look for open-air markets, as these are often of higher quality. Frozen fruits and vegetables are also great and have often been found to have a better-preserved nutrient profile than fresh fruits!

Examples of superfoods:

- Salmon and salmon oil are high in omegas 3 and 6, but be aware that the amount can be too high! Don't add extra.

- Berries, fresh or frozen, high in antioxidants

- Kefir or live natural unsweetened yogurt, fermented, supports a healthy microbiome

- Fermented vegetables - probiotics to support the microbiome. These can be added in small quantities to most recipes without unbalancing them

- Leafy greens provide a range of vitamins & phytonutrients

- Spirulina can boost the immune system and is great for a range of minerals and trace elements

- Turmeric is great for all sorts, including reducing inflammation, and is an excellent source of minerals. We use it often as it is also very affordable for balancing certain minerals in recipes.

- Nuts and seeds—(Incidentally, all men are recommended to have a Brazil nut each day for selenium, which is implicated in reducing prostate cancer!)

- A range of different oils - always try and source the highest quality cold-pressed versions

- Legumes are high in fiber and support gut health, but they are not advisable for puppies under 50% adult weight.

Ingredient exchanges

Any alteration of ingredients, even those you might consider similar, will impact the nutritional balance of a recipe. With such a wide range of recipes, we hope you can find a good collection of favorites for which you can source all the ingredients either locally or online. In particular, as mentioned, you will want to find a source for offal and organ meat. Be aware, though, that switching one animal source for another is not secure from a nutrient point of view. For example, lamb and beef liver have surprisingly different nutrient profiles, so avoid such switches where possible. Certainly, don't consider them a long-term solution.

Tinned mollusks, oysters, etc., are another ingredient you may not be familiar with, but they are very helpful at providing a range of important minerals, so you will see them in our recipes. If they are not stocked in your local store, you should find them readily online.

For any ingredients you cannot find in your local stores, try looking online before giving up on a recipe. Things you might not be familiar with, such as rice bran, certain mushrooms, and game meats - have fun looking for them! You may be surprised to find them in local stores you didn't even know existed, as people from different cultural backgrounds may cook regularly with ingredients we are not familiar with. I had never heard of chitterlings until I started feeding them to my dogs, but they are a popular dish down south, and you can get them in Walmart, so now they feature in our human dinner menus, too!

You have no doubt gathered by now that it is pretty important not to tamper with the recipes. Don't be tempted to add an extra spoon of this or an extra ounce of that. The individual nutrients may have fantastic benefits within the balanced diet, but excess can be as harmful as deficiency in some cases. If you are missing an ingredient, try another recipe. Missing a nutrient once or twice a week is not likely to cause harm, but bear in mind a puppy's growth phase is short and fast with no second chance. Do the best you can, and you will be repaid many times over with health and vitality in your adult dog for many more years.

Don't forget you also have a free personalized recipe opportunity. Once you know what your puppy's preferences are and which ingredients you can or can't source, head over to get your tailored recipe at www.ridgehilldogs.com/free-recipe

Allergies, sensitivities and intolerances

Some dogs have intolerances or allergies to certain foods, and as with humans, these incidents are on the rise. When your puppy first comes home, maintain its diet unchanged until you have seen your vet and the puppy has settled.

Switch to homemade food gradually over a week or more. Start by mixing your homemade with their existing diet at a ratio of no more than 25:75, then 50:50, then 75:25, until by the end of a week, at the quickest, they are 100% homemade. Keep a poop journal and slow down the switch if the pup suffers any diarrhea. Better to take your time and avoid the infection risk that can come with intestinal stress.

Intolerances or allergies usually show as an itchy rash, yeasty ears or paws (leading to head shaking or paw chewing), or an upset tummy. If you have concerns, talk to your vet.

To identify an allergy, you can either request testing from your vet or try an exclusion diet process. Most are related to proteins, so start there. To identify via exclusion, reduce protein variety for a few days to one single animal protein source at a time and watch for the resurgence of symptoms. If you do not identify any protein problem, add other ingredients, one at a time, and monitor and keep a diary.

Common culprits: Chicken, Treats, Gluten, and Dairy. There are only a few treats in this book, as treats are an entire subject and book unto themselves (coming soon!).. There are limited dairy products in the low-purine recipes but very few elsewhere, as dairy is high in fat and, therefore, challenging to balance overall.

Once you identify the problem food, talk to your vet about an appropriate swap or use that as the opportunity to get your personalized recipe. We will omit the problem ingredient(s).

Dalmatians (non-NUA) and dogs with hyperuricosuria [59,60,61]

Sadly, such dogs cannot have any secreting organ meat and must keep to a low purine diet, which is tricky to balance for puppies. If you have read the foregoing, you will appreciate the need for us to use certain mineral supplements instead of organ meats in these recipes. While we could develop a wide range of breed or disease-specific recipes, this book simply can't cover everything - maybe we'll write another on that topic. But as NUA Dalmatian breeders, we must find room for Spotties or be ostracized by our support group, who have inspired us to write this book in the first place! Therefore, you will find several specific low-purine recipes in each growth section. These are perfectly balanced and healthy for other puppies, too.

Toxic for dogs:

Cocoa, caffeine, alcohol, grapes, raisins, sultanas, xylitol, avocados, onions, and macadamia nuts should be avoided at all times.

There have been recent rumors that avocado flesh is safe for dogs, but research shows it causes gut irritation, vomiting, diarrhea, respiratory distress, congestion, fluid accumulation around tissues of the heart, and even death, so it is another dangerous rumor. I'm afraid. Macadamia nuts contain an unknown toxin, not simply their high-fat value. The toxic dose is very variable, so some dogs can eat quite a lot while others very little before becoming symptomatically unwell. Garlic is less dangerous than onions but still has a negative effect on the blood. There is insufficient dog-specific research to know if the benefits from garlic outweigh the risks. So, particularly for puppies, we would not choose to take such an unquantified risk; therefore, there is no garlic in any of the recipes. [36,37]

Recipe preparation and cooking (or not?!)

Raw? Cooked? Processing? What when and why?

One of the biggest debates so far in the book! Why is this so emotive, and how can answers be so challenging to establish? Ok, so let's ask the big questions most people have, and then we'll discuss why many of the answers remain so elusive

- Is raw healthier than cooked?

- Is homemade healthier than commercially produced?

- Is feeding mainly raw meat healthier than feeding commercial packet food?

Hhhmmmm, are these even the right questions? You see, it is tricky to specify the exact questions in people's minds, and each one is distinctly different. So, instead, let's try talking about the components of the questions—the issues if you like. Then maybe we can see how they might connect and how research may or may not have anything to help us.

Let's take the subject of raw feeding. What does this mean to you? To many, it is a predominantly uncooked diet of meat. Is cooking the issue? Is the type of meat the issue? Do dogs need vegetables? How are raw food diets balanced? Is this quantifiably measured?

Meat raw or cooked? Cooking can mean anything from hard boiling and crispy roasting to light steaming or a quick sizzle. We know cooking can reduce certain nutrient values, but interestingly, it can also make some nutrients more bioavailable.

Homemade versus commercial? It all depends. If your idea of homemade puppy food is brown rice, chicken breast, and broccoli, then honestly, I would recommend that you switch as fast as possible to the most expensive kibble you can afford. Think of a toddler. Would they be healthier on homemade bread with homemade strawberry jam and fresh homemade butter if that is all they ate daily or on packets and tins of pre-prepared nutritionally balanced baby food? As cynical as I am, I would put my money on the baby food. But comparing those jars of baby food to cooking or preparing a wide range of stews, curries, fruit muesli mixes, and mixed organic salads alongside some fresh bread and jam is a completely different picture – but both come under the banner of homemade meals. Do you see the challenges here?

And who is researching the answers to these questions for dogs and puppies? No-one really. The research - as you can see from the foregoing reference materials- has to be controlled precisely by its very nature, which means refined isolated compounds are being looked at individually. Assessing the holistic benefits of a wide-ranging and balanced homemade diet would require a huge population-based study of dogs and puppies, but who would fund such a study?

When you look for scientific research to answer these questions, the studies basically say things like 'there is a paucity of data, ' 'insufficient studies, ' 'more research required,' etc. We cannot see how we can expect institutions to fund studies to see if homemade diets, which don't earn anyone any profit, are in the best interest of our dog's long-term health when such a study would be virtually impossible to design, quantify, conduct and measure in any helpful or meaningful way.

Those reports that gather opinions through surveys I think give us some of the saddest results of all - most pet owners who respond are feeding out of fear. They either feed processed foods as they fear or distrust homemade/raw feeding, or they feed raw and homemade because they fear or distrust processed commercial foods. We find that idea most upsetting. Surely we can find a way to feed with confidence and joy? [62,68,69]

So what are we doing here, and why write this book?

- Research DOES tell us what nutrients puppies need to be healthy and what is seen to cause damage.

- Research DOES help us understand the importance of ratios and levels of different nutrients that impact puppies in the short, medium, and longer term.

- Research DOES demonstrate how ultra-processing damages nutrients and that nutrients in their natural whole-food forms are digested and absorbed differently and with more benefits compared to processed foods in human studies.

So there is a certain amount of extrapolation here, but I think most people would agree that if we can at least match the balance and availability of nutrients found in commercially highly processed dog foods and if we can do this predominantly via fresh wholefoods, then we can only be doing better—better than either serving up those processed foods or feeding an inadequate, albeit fresh, homemade diet.

Our goal is to give you the science, the tools, and the confidence to know you're providing the absolutely best possible nutrition for your puppy's health now and for a longer and healthier lifetime.

As to cooking v raw, the research is interesting. Consider meat and fish first. Research shows that the nutritional value of animal proteins, when gently cooked, is not significantly reduced, but the concentration of bio-available minerals increases. Vitamins are reduced with sustained or high-temperature cooking, such as frying, but not significantly at low steaming temperatures and short cooking durations. Oils and fatty acids are the most frequently observed changes, but not always negatively. The protein sources themselves are made more easily digestible by light cooking. So, when considering a wide range of research articles, there is no clear-cut negative for or against lightly cooking protein sources. [63,64,65,66,67]

The important thing from the point of view of balanced recipes is that **all your ingredients should be raw to start with, and only cook those recipes that have been balanced for cooking.** You need to control the cooking method in order to know that your end nutrient profile will match that of the recipe. Cooking will affect water content and, therefore, impact the final weight. So, for example, the amount of copper per gram of a completed recipe may rise per ounce/gram as you cook, but that won't matter because we have balanced the recipe to match the cooking method in the instructions.

Meat & fish

So, for you to decide whether you cook your animal proteins or not, here are our thoughts for what they are worth:

- If you are happy leaving meat and fish raw, then no problem. You can choose from both the cooked and uncooked recipes and save yourself time and washing up.

- If you wish to cook, that is also no big problem. Just ensure you only choose a cooked recipe.

- Why choose one over the other? Personal preference concerns over storage and handling large quantities of uncooked meat, perhaps, or how you want to store extra portions. There could be many reasons, but we don't feel nutrition is the main one when it comes to animal-based protein sources as long as you don't cook them too hard, for too long, or too hot. Your cooking method options are given in each recipe. Don't make any fat smoke, as that is damaging.

- Pork is safer cooked due to a small risk of a potential parasite, but other than that, we have not encountered any peer-reviewed scientific studies or research that lead us to feel strongly about this raw/cooked subject either way.

- Eggs—Considering the biotin discussion in Chapter 4, we recommend cooking egg whites if they form more than about 10% of any recipe.

Vegetable and other ingredient preparation & cooking

There are other very different considerations when it comes to veggies and plant-based items, which we use to balance nutrients in a puppy's diet.

For this, it would be helpful to have a brief biology lesson on the very basics of dog digestion. Puppies have a very much shorter and simpler digestive tract compared to humans. Our transit time for food to pass through our guts is from about 24 hours to 3 days. It is more like 6 to 24 hours or maybe 30 hours in puppies at most. They can break down animal cell membranes, meaning they can digest meats and fish, but they cannot break down plant cell walls. This means that for them to access the fantastic nutrients inside vegetables, nuts, seeds, or anything not animal in origin, we have to break these walls down for them. If you don't do this, they cannot benefit, and the plant-based ingredients, with all their goodness, will simply pass straight through. So feeding chunks of raw carrots to a puppy, you will see those little chunks come through in the poo, which means they got no nutritional value from it.

In fact, poop watching is a good way to see what is not getting digested, but it's very hard to see tiny bits like seeds, and anyone passing by as you scrutinize your pooch's poops is likely to think you're losing it. But jokes aside, you should keep a watchful eye on poop consistency, color, and general content to give you an early warning if something is not quite right. I feel another book is needed!

If you really want to go to town and make everything ultra-bio available, you can juice all the vegetable and fruit elements of a recipe and recombine the juice and pulp. I confess we do this for our young-stage puppies. It is a little more work, but with a decent juicer, we do batches, and I know that for those first few months, they are getting the best of the best. After that, we get a little laxer and might grate, finely chop, and/or steam the veggies, but sometimes that actually takes longer than just putting them through the juicer. The aim is to partially digest and break down those cell walls so all the nutrients can be absorbed in that short puppy gut transit time. Another similar route is to blend all the fruit and veg. in a big jug blender. You will likely need to add water, which can make the meals a bit large, but high water content is not negative and helps ensure good hydration, particularly in warmer seasons or areas. Be aware this will, of course, impact kcals per ounce/gram, so adjust portions accordingly.

Mushrooms always need to be cooked to make their nutrients bioavailable, but again, there is no need to cook them hard. Just chop and then lightly saute until soft. Chopping alone is not enough with mushrooms.

Chop nuts and grind seeds. When using an electric chopper, try not to get carried away. Don't allow nuts to get hot. While creating nut butter is not a major problem, it tends to lead to heat, which starts to degrade the fatty acids, and we want to preserve their nutrient value as much as possible.

If you mix seeds with nuts in a chopper, the seeds won't get chopped as they are too small and hard. You'll end up with a nut butter with seeds in it. It's delicious spread on toast for breakfast but not great for your pup as the seed nutrients remain sealed inside their hard casing.

Don't cook any of the oils (including nuts and seeds) as it is hard to regulate temperature, and it doesn't take much temperature to damage the beneficial activity of oils and their component fatty acids.

Kitchen equip & utensils

A Kitchen Scale is an Essential

I know you may not be accustomed to measuring in grams, but it is essential for these recipes to be accurately formulated. You will need a good set of kitchen scales. Ideally, you will find a set with two weighing platforms: one to weigh a big bowl up to 8kg and a second platform (or different scale) that goes down to 0.1g divisions for weighing micro-ingredients such as salt.

Other items you will find useful:

- The best cold press juicer you can afford if you intend to juice veggie and fruit components

- Big jug blender with a long motor guarantee - we've burnt out a few!

- Steamer to lightly cook ingredients while maintaining nutrients. Nutritionally, it is the best of the cooking options.

- Slow cooker. Great way to keep things easy, but we use ours more for us than the dogs

- Food processor. Saves a lot of time chopping. Can often get a nut chopper and seed (or coffee) grinder attachment

- Grinder for seeds and chopper for nuts if not on your food processor

- Meat grinder for mincing offal to enable effective distribution throughout the recipe

- The usual collection of chopping boards—it's good practice to have one for raw fish/meat and another for veggies or one for puppies only (not used for human food).

- A large mixing bowl, tub, or small bucket is needed for effective mixing of bulk batch ingredients. We have an old-fashioned wash tub as we tend to mix 30kg+ at a time, but most of these recipes are in the 6-7kg range as they are sized to 10,000kcals.

Recipe instructions

Enjoy creating these wonderful healthy meals knowing you are giving your puppy the best possible start in life

Each recipe has its own method provided, but here are some general instructions for preparing puppy food. Please weigh and measure all ingredients as carefully as possible to ensure the correct balance of all nutrients. Please read the recipe preparation section in Chapter 8.

Meat & fish:

- Cut some into suitable bite-sized pieces and grind the rest to end up with a mix of roughly 50:50 chunks & ground meat

- Preferably grind offal and any small quantity items to assist in effective distribution

- Leave raw or cook as per the recipe

Eggs:

- Add to the mix raw or lightly poach to ideally cook the white and leave the yolk runny.

- If you're making a large batch, crack the yolks into the mix and keep the whites separate to cook before adding them.

Vegetables, choose one of these methods to suit you and your puppy:

- Pass any fruit and vegetables through a juicer, then recombine the pulp and the juice. Or

- Blend fruit and veg. - Add as much water as needed to get it moving in the blender. Or

- Cut any fruit and veg into suitably sized pieces for your puppy and lightly steam until just soft. Or

- Finely chop or grate the fruit and vegetables and leave raw.

- Any herbs can simply be finely chopped and not cooked

Please don't cook any of the following.

Nuts & seeds:
- Chop any nuts

- Grind seeds in a coffee grinder or similar.

Any supplements:

- If in tablet form, add to the seeds for grinding.

- If in capsules, open the capsules and tip the contents into the mix.

- If powder, simply measure straight into the mixing bowl.

Oils, brans & meals:

- Measure and add directly to the mixing bowl.

Mix the recipe together as thoroughly as possible. Take your time to evenly distribute the ingredients. Now, you are ready to store and label.

Storage and portion calculation

Storage methods & containers and importance of labeling

Each recipe is for 10,000 kcal worth of puppy food. For a middle-of-the-range puppy, this is likely to be about a week of meals, but if you have a small breed, you can half or even quarter the ingredients, and with larger breeds, double up or more. As you complete each recipe and prepare for storage, you need to look at the kcals/ounce/100g given in the recipe data section. You may need to recalculate this value if you have introduced water or exchanged a recipe ingredient. To calculate yourself:

- Weigh the full bowl

- Deduct the weight of the bowl to find the total recipe weight

- Divide this weight in grams by 100 - call this A

- Total recipe kcals - 10,000 unless you have halved or doubled, etc

- Divide 10,000 by A

- The answer is how many kcals per 3.5oz/100g of recipe mix

- Divide the entire mix into whatever size batches are most convenient for you to store, but label them all with this kcal per 100g value.

- When you come to serve a meal, you will know approximately how many kcals your puppy needs and can weigh out a portion accordingly. See the Growth Rate section in Chapter 6 for more info on how to calculate portion sizes for your pup and practice BCS as a matter of habit.

Think about how you prefer to store it. You can keep meals fresh in a good fridge for several days, but freezing them for 3-6 months effectively saves quality. Maybe freeze in small batches if you have enough time to make several recipes and, in this way, create a library of different meals in the freezer. Don't defrost more than a few days at a time, and always adjust portion size to your puppy's current condition. Don't just feed that extra bit because it was left over and end up with a fat puppy.

Fridge - You can store for approx. 4-5 days between 36F & 40F (3 to 5C)

Freezer—Any fish-based recipes can be frozen for up to 3 months and meat-based recipes for up to 6 months. Mark each container with the date and kcal/oz or 100g. Keep rotating your stocks. We have big freezers out in a workshop where we can store ingredients, and we store completed recipes in our kitchen freezer, but we have multiple medium/large dogs, so this may not be helpful to you.

Kilner jar preservation - You need a pressure cooker, preserving jars & lids. Useful to make homemade dog food on holiday or store bulk batches without a freezer. Once opened, jars need refrigerating and use within a few days. You don't need to precook any ingredients. Simply fill each jar with raw recipe mixture and pressure cook/preserve. Don't forget to label them and only use the cooked recipes. Omit any oils and add them fresh on the day.

Suppliers

As suppliers change and alter their offerings, it seems more sensible to give you a live list that we can keep up to date. You will find this on our website at www.ridgehilldogs.com/suppliers.

After reading the nutritional guide, I hope you have feedback to share or questions to ask. Please submit a review on Amazon so that we can understand what you and other like-minded owners would like to see in future updated editions.

You can get a free copy of any future edition and also free copies of pre-publishing versions of our books by signing up for our newsletter at www.ridgehilldogs.com

Academic research papers

Resources for the foregoing section

Most of these citations are academic research papers; some are written for the general public, and some are regulatory documents written for industry. Some are fully available to the public, and some are partly available such that you can read an abstract, but the full text may only be available either through an institutional subscription or by paying a one-off fee. You can gain free access to some of these non-public articles by registering with the relevant research database without paying a fee. For others, you may be able to request access at your local library.

1. https://www.waltham.com/s3media/2020-05/walthampocketbookofpuppynutritionandcare.pdf

2. University of California, Davis School of Veterinary Medicine 'Homemade dog food recipes can be a risky business, study finds' (15 July 2013)

3. Wu, G. (2024). Roles of Nutrients in the Brain Development, Cognitive Function, and Mood of Dogs and Cats. In: Wu, G. (eds) Nutrition and Metabolism of Dogs and Cats. Advances in Experimental Medicine and Biology, vol 1446. Springer, Cham.

4. Veterinary Technician 27 PUPPY POWER! OPTIMAL NUTRITION FOR LIFE Kara M. Burns, MS, MEd, LVT President, Academy of Veterinary Nutrition Technicians Wamego, KS

5. A Research Update for the Veterinarian from Affinity Petcare. Puppy nutrition Isabelle Jeusette, DVM, PhD Victor Romano, DVM

6. Gislaine Cristina Bill Kaelle, Taís Silvino Bastos, Renata Bacila Morais dos Santos de Souza, Eduarda Lorena Fernandes, Simone Gisele de Oliveira, Ananda Portella Félix,

Different starch sources result in distinct responses to diets digestibility, fecal microbiota, and fermentative metabolites, and postprandial glycemic response in dogs, Animal Feed Science and Technology, Volume 306, 2023, 115822, ISSN 0377-8401,

7. The Veterinary Nurse, Nutrition for puppies, 02 November 2018, CLINICAL Clare Hemmings

8. The North American Veterinary Conference – 2005 Proceedings 602 IMPROVING PUPPY TRAINABILITY THROUGH NUTRITION Allan J. Lepine, PhD The Iams Company

9. Lanska DJ. Chapter 30: historical aspects of the major neurological vitamin deficiency disorders: the water-soluble B vitamins. Handb Clin Neurol. 2010;95:445-76. doi: 10.1016/S0072-9752(08)02130-1. PMID: 19892133.

10. http://hdl.handle.net/1854/LU-2987804. Bone disorder in copper-deficient puppies.

11. Journal article: American Journal of Physiology, 1951, Vol. 167, 766. Author: J. H. Baxter

12. Larkin, E.C., Rao, G.A. (1990). Importance of Fetal and Neonatal Iron: Adequacy for Normal Development of Central Nervous System. In: Dobbing, J. (eds) Brain, Behaviour, and Iron in the Infant Diet. Springer, London. https://doi.org/10.1 007/978-1-4471-1766-7_5

13. VanSteenhouse JL. Free radicals: relation to tissue damage – a review. Vet Clin Pathol. 1987;16:29-35. 2. Jewell DE, Toll PW, Wedekind KJ, et al.

Effect of increasing dietary antioxidants on concentrations of vitamin E and total alkenals in serum of dogs and cats. Vet Ther. 2000;1:264-272. 3. Wedekind KJ, Zicker S, Lowry S, et al.

Antioxidant status of adult beagles is affected by dietary antioxidant intake. J Nutr. 2002;132:1658S-1660S. 4. Chew BS, Park JS, Wong TS, et al.

Dietary -carotene stimulates cell-mediated and humoral immune response in dogs. J Nutr. 2000;130:1910-1913. 5. Heaton P, Reed CF, Mann SJ, et al.

Role of dietary antioxidants to protect against DNA damage in adult dogs. J Nutr. 2002;132:1720S-1724S.

14. Ana Margarida Pereira, Carlo Pinna, Giacomo Biagi, Claudio Stefanelli, Margarida R G Maia, Elisabete Matos, Marcela A Segundo, António J M Fonseca, Ana Rita J Cabrita, Supplemental selenium source on gut health: insights on fecal microbiome and fermentation products of growing puppies, FEMS Microbiology Ecology, Volume 96, Issue 11, November 2020, fiaa212,

15. A BEHAVIORIST'S GUIDE TO NATURAL THERAPEUTICS. Gary M. Landsberg, BSc, DVM, DACVB, DE-CAWBM. North Toronto Veterinary Behaviour Specialty Clinic, Thornhill, ON, Canada

16. Fieten, H., Leegwater, P.A.J., Watson, A.L. et al. Canine models of copper toxicosis for understanding mammalian copper metabolism. Mamm Genome 23, 62–75 (2012). https://doi.org/10.1007/s00335-011-9378-7

17. Beynen AC, 2020. Copper in dog food

18. http://hdl.handle.net/1854/LU-2987804. Bone disorder in copper-deficient puppies.

19.Journal article: American Journal of Physiology, 1951, Vol. 167, 766 Author: J. H. Baxter

20. Morris PJ, Salt C, Raila J, et al. Safety evaluation of vitamin A in growing dogs. British Journal of Nutrition. 2012;108(10):1800-1809. doi:10.1017/S0007114512000128

21. Effects of low phosphorus supply on the availability of calcium and phosphorus, and musculoskeletal development of growing dogs of two different breeds B. Kiefer-Hecker, E. Kienzle, B. Dobenecker

22. Influence of dietary calcium and phosphorus content in a fixed ratio on growth and development in Great Danes Susan D. Lauten

23. Dietary imbalances in a large breed puppy, leading to compression fractures, vitamin D deficiency, and suspected nutritional secondary hyperparathyroidism Moran Tal, Jacqueline M. Parr, Shawn MacKenzie, and Adronie Verbrugghe

24. Relation of synthetic folic acid to niacin deficiency in dogs. Journal article: Arch. Biochem., 1946, Vol. 11, 363-369 Authors: W. A. Krehl, N. Torbet, J. De La Huerga, C. A. Elvehjem Affiliation: Coll. Agric., Univ. Wisconsin, Madison

25. https://europeanpetfood.org/wp-content/uploads/2022/03/Updated-Nutritional-Guidelines.pdf

26. https://www.aafco.org/resources/guides-and-manuals/

27. https://www.aafco.org/wp-content/uploads/2023/01/Pet_Food_Report_2014_Annual-Appendix_A.pdf

28. https://animalnutrition.org/nrc_reports

29. PhD, Nancy R. Cox DVM, PhD, William R. Brawner Jr DVM, PhD, Susan A. Goodman DVM, MS, John T. Hathcock DVM, MS, Ronald D. Montgomery DVM, MS, Steven A. Kincaid DVM, PhD, Nancy E. Morrison MS, Joseph S. Spano DVM, PhD, Allan. J. Lepine PhD, Gregory A. Reinhart PhD, and Henry J. Baker DVM

30. https://www.waltham.com/resources/puppy-growth-charts

31. https://www.waltham.com/s3media/2020-05/completeguidetowalthampuppygrowthcharts_final.pdf

32. Yasmine Belkaid, Timothy W. Hand, Role of the Microbiota in Immunity and Inflammation, Cell,Volume 157, Issue 1, 2014, Pages 121-141, ISSN 0092-8674

33. ISSN 1392-2130. VETERINARIJA IR ZOOTECHNIKA (Vet Med Zoot). T. 61 (83). 2013 14 EFFECT OF PROBIOTIC PREPARATIONS ON THE GROWTH AND ASSIMILATION OF NUTRITIVE SUBSTANCES IN DIFFERENT BREEDS OF PUPPIES

34.Effects of supplementary feeding complex-probiotic-preparation on growth performance, intestinal motility and intestinal barrier function of puppies.

Journal article: Chinese Journal of Animal Nutrition, 2019, Vol. 31, No. 9, 4242-4250 ref. 25

Authors: Lu Jiang Lu Jiang, Zhu DaoXian Zhu DaoXian, Lu PengFei Lu PengFei, Zhang DongHao Zhang DongHao, Liu Jing Liu Jing, Fu HongQing Fu HongQing Affiliation: Department of Pet Science and Technology, Jiangsu Agri-Animal Husbandry Vocational College, Taizhou 225300, China Author Email: vetlj@163.com

35. A multi-strain probiotic promoted recovery of puppies from gastroenteritis in a randomized, double-blind, placebo-controlled study Authors: Molina, Rosa A.; Villar, Marcela D'Urso; Miranda, María H.; Maldonado, Natalia C.; Vignolo, Graciela M.; Nader-Macías, María E.F. Source: The Canadian Veterinary Journal, Volume 64, Number 7, July 2023, pp. 666-673(8) Publisher: Canadian Veterinary Medical Association

36. Interdisc Toxicol. 2009; Vol. 2(3): 169–176. doi: 10.2478/v10102-009-0012-4 Published online in: www.setox.eu/intertox & www.versita.com/science/medicine/it/ Copyright©2009 SlovakToxicologySocietySETOX

37. Some food toxic for pets Putative avocado toxicity in two dogs Buoro, I.B.J.; Nyamwange, S.B.; Chai, D.; Munyua, S.M.; Verwoerd, Daniel Wynand

38 Diane A. Hirakawa, David H. Baker, Lysine requirement of growing puppies fed practical and purified diets, Nutrition Research, Volume 6, Issue 5, 1986, Pages 527-538, ISSN 0271-5317

39. RT Journal Article A1 Coon, Craig N A1 Varney, Jessica L A1 Fowler, Jason W A1 Weil, Jordan T A1 Boggess, Mary Ann T1 236 Determination of amino acid requirements of lysine and tryptophan of >14 wk old growing Labrador retriever puppies using the indicator amino acid oxidation technique JF Journal of Animal Science JO J Anim Sci YR 2019 DO 10.1093/jas/skz258.124 VO 97 IS Supplement_3 SP 59 OP 60 SN 0021-8812

40. Gail L. Czarnecki, Diane A. Hirakawa, David H. Baker, Antagonism of Arginine by Excess Dietary Lysine in the Growing Dog, The Journal of Nutrition, Volume 115, Issue 6, 1985, Pages 743-752, ISSN 0022-3166, https://doi.org/10.1093/jn/115.6.743. (https://www.sciencedirect.com/science/article/pii/S0022316623075594)

41. Hilda F. Wiese, Mildred J. Bennett, Edmund Coon, William Yamanaka, Lipid Metabolism of Puppies as Affected by Kind and Amount of Fat and of Dietary Carbohydrate, The Journal of Nutrition, Volume 86, Issue 3, 1965, Pages 271-280, ISSN 0022-3166, https://doi.org/10.1093/jn/86.3.271. (https://www.sciencedirect.com/science/article/pii/S0022316623146426)

42. Sarah Colombini, Canine Zinc-Responsive Dermatosis, Veterinary Clinics of North America: Small Animal Practice, Volume 29, Issue 6, 1999, Pages 1373-1383, ISSN 0195-5616, https://doi.org/10.1016/S0195-5616(99)50133-2. (https://www.sciencedirect.com/science/article/pii/S0195561699501332)

43.Yongqing Hou, Guoyao Wu, Nutritionally Essential Amino Acids, Advances in Nutrition, Volume 9, Issue 6, 2018, Pages 849-851, ISSN 2161-8313, https://doi.org/10.1093/advances/nmy054. (https://www.sciencedirect.com/science/article/pii/S216183132201273X)

44. J Physiol. 1941 Jun 30; 99(4): 467–486. doi: 10.1113/jphysiol.1941.sp003916 PMCID: PMC1394093 PMID: 16995266

45. Lewis ED, Meydani SN, Wu D. Regulatory role of vitamin E in the immune system and inflammation. IUBMB Life. 2019 Apr;71(4) 487-494. doi:10.1002/iub.1976. PMID: 30501009; PMCID: PMC7011499.

46. Relation of synthetic folic acid to niacin deficiency in dogs. Journal article: Arch. Biochem., 1946, Vol. 11, 363-369 Authors: W. A. Krehl, N. Torbet, J. De La Huerga, C. A. Elvehjem Affiliation: Coll. Agric., Univ. Wisconsin, Madison

47. Choline deficiency studies in dogs. Journal article: Journal of Laboratory and Clinical Medicine, 1944, Vol. 29, 1109-1122 Authors: J. M. Mckibbin, S. Thayer, F. J. Stare Affiliation: Dept. Nutrit., Harvard Sch. Pub. Health, Boston

48.https://www.researchgate.net/profile/Anton-Beynen/publication/351624362_Beynen_AC_2021_Choline_in_dog_fo od/links/60a1e967458515c265994ba5/Beynen-AC-2021-Choline-in-dog-food.pdf accessed 6/5/24

49. Delaney, S. J., and Dzanis, D. A. (2018). Safety of vitamin K, and its use in pet foods. Journal of the American Veterinary Medical Association 252, 5, 537-542, available from: <https://doi.org/10.2460/javma.252.5.537> [Accessed 06 May 2024]

50. The Effects of Varying Dietary Potassium on the Electrocardiogram and Blood Electrolytes in Young Dogs

Ichio ONO, Tokuo HUKUOKA, Isao ONODERA □□□□ □□□□□ □□□ 1964 □ 5 □ 3 □ p. 272-286 DOI https://doi.org/10. 1536/ihj.5.272

51. Felder, C., Robillard, J., Roy, S. et al. Severe Chloride Deficiency in the Neonate: The Canine Puppy as an Animal Model. Pediatr Res 21, 497–501 (1987). https://doi.org/10.1203/00006450-198705000-00015

52. Effects of Magnesium-Deficient Diet Upon Puppies JOSEPH J. VITALE, EARL E. HELLERSTEIN, MOTOOMI NAKAMURA and BERNARD LOWN Originally published1 Mar 1961https://doi.org/10.1161/01.RES.9.2.387Circulati on Research. 1961;9:387–394

53. MDPI and ACS Style Jacuńska, W.; Biel, W.; Witkowicz, R.; Maciejewska-Markiewicz, D.; Piątkowska, E. Comparison of Key Nutrient Content of Commercial Puppy Foods with Canine Dietary Requirements. Appl. Sci. 2023, 13, 11791. https://doi.org/10.3390/app132111791

54. Effect of Chronic Nutritional Iron Deficiency on the Small Intestinal Disaccharidase Activities of Growing Dogs A. Victor Hoffbrand and Selwyn A. BroitmanView all authors and affiliations Volume 130, Issue 2

https://doi.org/10.3181/00379727-130-33615

55. Naigamwalla DZ, Webb JA, Giger U. Iron deficiency anemia. Can Vet J. 2012 Mar;53(3):250-6. PMID: 22942439; PMCID: PMC3280776.

56. J. H. Freeland-Graves, T. Y. Mousa, and N. Sanjeevi, in Manganese in Health and Disease, ed. L. Costa and M. Aschner, The Royal Society of Chemistry, 2014, ch. 2, pp. 34-75.

57. Castillo, V. A., Pisarev, M. A., Lalia, J. C., Rodriguez, M. S., Cabrini, R. L., & Marquez, A. G. (2001). Nutrition: Commercial diet induced hypothyroidism due to high iodine. A histological and radiological analysis. Veterinary Quarterly, 23(4), 218–223. https://doi.org/10.1080/01652176.2001.9695117

58. Ana Margarida Pereira, Carlo Pinna, Giacomo Biagi, Claudio Stefanelli, Margarida R G Maia, Elisabete Matos, Marcela A Segundo, António J M Fonseca, Ana Rita J Cabrita, Supplemental selenium source on gut health: insights on fecal microbiome and fermentation products of growing puppies, FEMS Microbiology Ecology, Volume 96, Issue 11, November 2020, fiaa212, https://doi.org/10.1093/femsec/fiaa212

59. Sorenson, J. L., & Ling, G. V. (1993). Metabolic and genetic aspects of urate urolithiasis in Dalmatians. Journal of the American Veterinary Medical Association, 203(6), 857-862. Retrieved May 7, 2024, from https://doi.org/10.2460/javma.19 93.203.06.0857

60. Mutations in the SLC2A9 Gene Cause Hyperuricosuria and Hyperuricemia in the Dog Danika Bannasch, Noa Safra,Amy Young,Nili Karmi,R. S. Schaible,G. V. Ling Published: November 7, 2008

https://doi.org/10.1371/journal.pgen.1000246

61.https://www.vettimes.co.uk/app/uploads/wp-post-to-pdf-enhanced-cache/1/overview-of-backcross-project-normal-uric-acid-in-dalmatians.pdf (accessed 7/5/24)

62. Genever Morgan, Nicola Williams, Vanessa Schmidt, Daisy Cookson, Carrie Symington, Gina Pinchbeck,

A Dog's Dinner: Factors affecting food choice and feeding practices for UK dog owners feeding raw meat-based or conventional cooked diets, Preventive Veterinary Medicine, Volume 208, 2022, 105741, ISSN 0167-5877, https://doi.org/10.1016/j.prevetmed.2022.105741. (https://www.sciencedirect.com/science/article/pii/S016758772200174X)

63. Oz, F. and Celik, T. (2015), Some Properties of Goose Meat. Journal of Food Processing and Preservation, 39: 2442-2454. https://doi.org/10.1111/jfpp.12494

64. Ersoy, B. (2011), Effects of cooking methods on the proximate, mineral and fatty acid composition of European eel (Anguilla anguilla). International Journal of Food Science & Technology, 46: 522-527. https://doi.org/10.1111/j.1365-2621.2010.02546.x

65. Oz, F., Aksu, M.I. and Turan, M. (2017), The Effects of Different Cooking Methods on Some Quality Criteria and Mineral Composition of Beef Steaks. Journal of Food Processing and Preservation, 41: e13008. https://doi.org/10.1111/jfpp.13008

66. M.J. Marchello, W.D. Slanger, D.B. Milne, A.G. Fischer, P.T. Berg, Nutrient composition of raw and cooked Bison bison, Journal of Food Composition and Analysis, Volume 2, Issue 2, 1989, Pages 177-185, ISSN 0889-1575, https://doi.org/10.1016/0889-1575(89)90079-3. (https://www.sciencedirect.com/science/article/pii/0889157589900793)

67. Jiaqiang Luo, Cheryl Taylor, Thomas Nebl, Ken Ng, Louise E. Bennett,

Effects of macro-nutrient, micro-nutrient composition and cooking conditions on in vitro digestibility of meat and aquatic dietary proteins, Food Chemistry, Volume 254, 2018, Pages 292-301, ISSN 0308-8146, https://doi.org/10.1016/j.foodchem.2018.01.164. (https://www.sciencedirect.com/science/article/pii/S0308814618301791)

68. Insights into dog owner perspectives on risks, benefits, and nutritional value of raw diets compared to commercial cooked diets Research articleVeterinary MedicineZoologyNutritionPublic Health Alysia Empert-Gallegos, Sally Hill, Philippa S. Yam

69. T Journal Article A1 Algya, Kiley M A1 Cross, Tzu-Wen L A1 Leuck, Kristen N A1 Kastner, Megan E A1 Baba, Toshiro A1 Lye, Lynn A1 de Godoy, Maria R C A1 Swanson, Kelly S T1 Apparent total-tract macronutrient digestibility, serum chemistry, urinalysis, and fecal characteristics, metabolites and microbiota of adult dogs fed extruded, mildly cooked, and raw diets1 JF Journal of Animal Science JO J Anim Sci YR 2018 DO 10.1093/jas/sky235 VO 96 IS 9 SP 3670 OP 3683 SN 0021-8812

Recipes

The recipes are split into growth stage sections.

Our first section is recipes suitable for puppies during and from weaning up to 50% of their adult weight. The second section is for puppies from 50% of their anticipated adult weight up to 80%, and again, the above categories are catered for. The third section covers 80% of adult weight up to adult, and the final bonus section includes an adult recipe, and 2 training treat recipes suitable for puppies and adults of any age.

Note that you can continue to use any recipes for a growth stage YOUNGER than your puppy but do not use recipes for OLDER puppies.

In each section, you will find 3 categories:

1. Recipes that are balanced if everything remains raw.

2. Recipes that are balanced, whether cooked or raw or if you cook only the meat and keep everything else raw.

3. Low purine recipes that are balanced and suitable for dogs with hyperuricosuria. These are perfectly healthy for any puppies, but as you will see, the range of ingredients is far more limited, so supplementation is greater by necessity. The individual recipes will tell you if they are raw or cooked recipes.

All the puppy names in the recipes are real dogs. Most of them are puppies we have raised and live wonderful, happy lives with their wonderful owners! We keep in touch and receive regular updates and photos, so we feel they remain part of the family. There are also a handful of "guest star" dogs belonging to other family members or friends that you will meet as you try out different recipes.

Please note. To formulate these recipes, we have used professional veterinary industry-leading software. We rely on the accuracy of data in the software database and, therefore, cannot guarantee the accuracy and completeness of the nutritional data we provide in the recipe reports. It is the best we have available, but it cannot be guaranteed. Furthermore, there is considerable natural variability of nutrients within natural products. Wherever you see Lysine* in the nutrient tables, please see Chapter 3 for further information.

All the recipes are formulated to give 10,000 kcals worth of finished puppy food. You will notice the recipes vary in kcal per ounce (or 100g), as provided in the data tables. This can help you choose a recipe. If you have a greedy puppy always looking for more, choose a lower kcal/oz recipe, as they can eat a larger bulk of food. If your pup often doesn't finish their dinner, try a higher kcal/oz recipe, as this will pack more nutrition into a smaller volume of food, making it more likely they will finish their dinner. See Chapter 5 to calculate portion sizes and track the growth rate for your puppy.

RAW. Puppies under 50% of their anticipated adult weight

Likely 14 weeks old and younger

These recipes have all been formulated and nutritionally balanced based on ingredients remaining raw. See Chapter 8 for more details about raw vs. cooking.

Puppy weight for these recipes is less than 50% of their final anticipated adult weight. This likely means your puppy is under 14-16 weeks old. See Chapter 5 for more information about different growth phases, growth charts, and how to score body condition.

In these early growth stage recipes, we have relied more heavily on bonemeal and less on ground bone to balance calcium and phosphorus. This is due to the more critical nature of the Ca, P quantities and ratio at this age. Ground chicken wings/backs/necks and similar sources of bone suitable for mincing are, by their very nature, more variable in bone content, so using bonemeal gives more precise control. However, I appreciate that some people prefer to rely on whole foods as much as possible, so some recipes in this growth stage include ground bones. This becomes more common as you move through the book to later growth-stage recipes.

Bella's Beef

& Blueberries

This beefy delight is a favorite when we are weaning puppies. Beef spleen is an excellent and digestible source of iron. We buy it frozen online, but if you struggle to source spleen, you can omit it and substitute 54mg of iron supplement to rebalance this recipe, although be aware that the kcal values will change.

Formulated to FEDIAF

Ingredients

4,050g (8lb 13oz) Ground beef (10% fat)

155g Beef liver, freeze-dried

43g Beef spleen

452g Fresh whole eggs (no shell)

362g Blueberries

137g Brazil nuts

127g Hempseed

141g Nutritional Yeast

85g Bonemeal

28g Spirulina, dried powder

28g Turmeric, dried powder

10g Kelp powder (I = 700mcg/g)

8.5g Salt, finely ground

19g Sunflower or Safflower oil

15g Cod liver oil

Please weigh all ingredients accurately.

To thoroughly mix the recipe, you will need a large mixing bowl, tub, or small bucket and a large, sturdy, long-handled spoon.

Method

1. Start by placing the ground beef base in your large bowl

2. Add the dried beef liver. Depending upon puppy size, this may need chopping, but suitably sized pieces add texture for your puppy to chew on.

3. Chop or grind the spleen to aid even distribution. Add to the bowl

4. Crack the whole fresh eggs straight into the bowl or separate the whites and poach those before adding them to avoid any potential biotin absorption concerns. (See Chapt. 8)

5. Add the whole blueberries; if you are helping yourself, ensure you allow that in your quantity!

6. Chop the Brazil nuts and grind the hemp seeds before adding them to the mix.

7. Add all the dry ingredients: bonemeal, spirulina, turmeric, kelp, and salt

8. Roughly mix the wet and dry ingredients in the bowl so that no dry powders remain visible

9. Add the sunflower and cod liver oils and thoroughly mix the entire batch.

10. Weigh out a suitably sized portion to serve to your puppy.

For the best long-term health, practice body condition scoring, use the growth charts, and try not to over- or underfeed. Refrigerate or freeze the remainder.

See Chapt. 5 for growth charts and portion sizing, Chapt. 6 for substitutions, Chapts. 8-10 for additional method details, tips, & advice, Chapt. 11 for storage info. and Chapt. 12 for online suppliers.

Nutritional Information

MACRONUTRIENT ANALYSIS			
Composition	As formulated	Dry Matter	% kcal
Protein	20.26%	53%	40%
Fat	11.78%	31%	56%
Ash	2.80%	7%	
Moisture	61.98%		
Fiber	1.23%	3%	
Net Carbs	1.95%	5%	4%
Sugars	1.24%	3%	2%
Starch	0.75%	2%	1%
Total			100%

MACRONUTRIENT INFORMATION				
				10,000
Total kcal in recipe				50
kcal / oz				807
kcal / lb				178
kcal / 100g				1,778
kcal / kg				

MINERALS				
	Unit	Min	Max	Recipe
Ca	g	2.5	4	2.8
P	g	2.25		2.73
Ca:P	ratio	1:1	1.8:1	1.03 : 1
K	g	1.1		2.2
Na	g	0.55		0.76
MG	g	0.1		0.27
Cl	g	0.83		1.01
Fe	mg	22	350	22.78
Cu	mg	2.75	7	6.32
Mn	mg	1.4	40	2.09
Zn	mg	25	70	25.14
I	mg	0.38	3	0.69
Se	mg	0.1		0.36

VITAMINS				
	Unit	Min	Max	Recipe
Vit A	IU	1,250		7799.63
Vit C	mg			0.8
Vit D	IU	138		331.52
Vit E	IU	12.5		12.69
Thiamine, B1	mg	0.45		10.49
Riboflavine, B2	mg	1.05		11.43
Niacin, B3	mg	3.4		76.6
Pantothenic Acid, B5	mg	3		8
B6 (Pyridoxine)	mg	0.3		9.92
Vit B12	mg	0.01		0.05
Folic Acid	mg	0.05		0.95
Choline	mg	425		555.69
Vit K1	mg			0.01
Biotin	mg			0.19

FATS				
	Unit	Min	Max	Recipe
Total	g	21.25		66.23
Saturated	g			21.41
Monounsaturated	g			24.95
Polyunsaturated	g			11.54
LA	g	3.25	16.25	8.73
ALA	g	0.2		1.32
AA	g	0.08		0.27
EPA	g			0.13
DPA	g			0.02
DHA	g			0.17
Omega-6/Omega-3	ratio			5.10 : 1
EPA + DHA	g	0.13		0.3

AMINO ACIDS				
	Unit	Min	Max	Recipe
Total protein	g	62.5		113.9
Tryptophan	g	0.58		0.8
Threonine	g	2.03		4.51
Isoleucine	g	1.63		5.11
Leucine	g	3.23		8.95
Lysine*	g	2.2	7*	8.78
Methionine	g	0.88		2.96
M - Cystine	g	1.75		4.35
Phenylalanine	g	1.63		4.72
P - Tyrosine	g	3.25		8
Valine	g	1.7		5.93
Arginine	g	2.05		7.68
Histidine	g	0.98		3.51
Purines	mg			524.03
Taurine	g			0.15

Bobo's Bison

& Catfish

Although Bison meat is expensive for many of us, it can be locally and affordably available directly from the ranch if you live near a Bison ranch. As variety is the spice of life, we put together this Bison recipe for those lucky pups in the right circumstances. (Hello to Bobo's parents, our friends in the Ozarks!)

Formulated to FEDIAF

Ingredients

4,076g Bison meat, lean

606g Chicken necks

394g Bison liver

233g Bison heart

933g Catfish

169g Oysters

727g Green leafy veg mix

149g Sunflower or Safflower seeds

37g Fennel seeds

55g Bonemeal

53g Turmeric powder

10g Salt

8g Kelp powder (I = 700mcg/g)

2,800mg Choline, e.g. 8 capsules at 350mg/cap

6mg Copper, e.g. 3 capsules at 2mg/cap

Please weigh all ingredients accurately.

This recipe requires a meat grinder that can cope with poultry bones.

You will need a large mixing bowl, tub, or small bucket and a large, sturdy, long-handled spoon to thoroughly mix the recipe.

Method

1. Chop about half the bison meat and half the catfish into bite-sized chunks and place in your mixing bowl.

2. Grind the rest of the bison and catfish, along with the chicken necks, liver, heart, and oysters, and add them to the bowl.

3. Chop and add the leafy greens, or if you have a juicer, run them through it and add both pulp and juice to the mix.

4. Chop the sunflower seeds and grind the fennel seeds before adding them

5. Now add all the dry powdered ingredients: bonemeal, turmeric, salt & kelp

6. Twist open supplement capsules and sprinkle the powder into the bowl

7. Thoroughly mix the entire recipe

8. Weigh out a suitably sized portion to serve your puppy, who is undoubtedly watching your every move!

For the best long-term health, practice body condition scoring, use the growth charts, and try not to over- or underfeed. Refrigerate or freeze the remainder.

See Chapt. 5 for growth charts and portion sizing, Chapt. 6 for substitutions, Chapts. 8-10 for additional method details, tips, & advice, Chapt. 11 for storage info. and Chapt. 12 for online suppliers.

Nutritional Information

MACRONUTRIENT ANALYSIS			
Composition	As formulated	Dry Matter	% kcal
Protein	17%	56%	44%
Fat	8%	28%	53%
Ash	2%	8%	
Moisture	70%		
Fiber	1%	3%	
Net Carbs	1%	4%	3%
Sugars	0%	1%	1%
Starch	1%	3%	2%
Total			100%

MACRONUTRIENT INFORMATION				
				10,000
Total kcal in recipe				38
kcal / oz				608
kcal / lb				134
kcal / 100g				1,341
kcal / kg				

MINERALS				
	Unit	Min	Max	Recipe
Ca	g	2.5	4	2.7
P	g	2.25		2.61
Ca:P	ratio	1:1	1.8:1	1.03 : 1
K	g	1.1		2.51
Na	g	0.55		0.82
MG	g	0.1		0.33
Cl	g	0.83		0.98
Fe	mg	22	350	22.86
Cu	mg	2.75	7	3.24
Mn	mg	1.4	40	2.57
Zn	mg	25	70	26.56
I	mg	0.38	3	0.54
Se	mg	0.1		0.15

VITAMINS				
	Unit	Min	Max	Recipe
Vit A	IU	1,250		10464.9
Vit C	mg			34.37
Vit D	IU	138		499.19
Vit E	IU	12.5		12.66
Thiamine, B1	mg	0.45		0.95
Riboflavine, B2	mg	1.05		2.4
Niacin, B3	mg	3.4		27.52
Pantothenic Acid, B5	mg	3		7.62
B6 (Pyridoxine)	mg	0.3		2.25
Vit B12	mg	0.01		0.04
Folic Acid	mg	0.05		0.24
Choline	mg	425		746.89
Vit K1	mg			0.32
Biotin	mg			0.06

FATS				
	Unit	Min	Max	Recipe
Total	g	21.25		62.68
Saturated	g			22.65
Monounsaturated	g			24.1
Polyunsaturated	g			8.69
LA	g	3.25	16.25	6.37
ALA	g	0.2		0.39
AA	g	0.08		0.28
EPA	g			0.19
DPA	g			0.15
DHA	g			0.33
Omega-6/Omega-3	ratio			7.08 : 1
EPA + DHA	g	0.13		0.52

AMINO ACIDS				
	Unit	Min	Max	Recipe
Total protein	g	62.5		124.53
Tryptophan	g	0.58		1.14
Threonine	g	2.03		5.3
Isoleucine	g	1.63		5.73
Leucine	g	3.23		10.12
Lysine*	g	2.2	7*	10.56
Methionine	g	0.88		3.22
M - Cystine	g	1.75		4.74
Phenylalanine	g	1.63		5.07
P - Tyrosine	g	3.25		9.23
Valine	g	1.7		6.33
Arginine	g	2.05		8.09
Histidine	g	0.98		3.79
Purines	mg			613.32
Taurine	g			0.24

Sadie's Salmon

& Seafood

Salmon varies significantly in price according to region and season, but when it is readily available and affordable, we stock up our freezer. It is nutritious and delicious for both our dogs and ourselves. In fact, this entire recipe is startlingly similar to a Salmon and Broccoli bake my husband loves me to make! (Just leave out the bonemeal and add a cream sauce, haha.)

Formulated to FEDIAF

Ingredients

4,215g Salmon

1,264g Broccoli

948g Oysters

211g Egg, whole, no shell

211g Almonds

211g Flaxseed or Chia seeds

185g Turmeric powder

105g Bonemeal

2g Kelp powder (I = 700mcg/g)

Please weigh all ingredients accurately.

You will need a large mixing bowl, tub, or small bucket and a large, sturdy, long-handled spoon to thoroughly mix the recipe.

Method

1. Grind approx. half the salmon and chop the rest into bite-sized chunks to suit your puppy's size. Place in a large mixing bowl.

2. Put the broccoli through a juicer and add juice and pulp into the bowl. If you don't have a juicer, chop the crown finely and grate the stems.

3. Grind or finely chop the oysters to aid even distribution and add to the bowl.

4. Crack the eggs straight into the mix. There is no need to poach the whites, as they are a small proportion of the total recipe.

5. Chop the almonds and grind the seeds before adding them to the bowl. If using a mechanical chopper, don't try to chop nuts and seeds at the same time, as the seeds will not get touched before the almonds turn to butter.

6. Now add the dry powders: turmeric, bonemeal, and kelp.

7. Mix thoroughly

Weigh out a suitably sized portion to serve your furball in residence—I am talking about your puppy, not your partner! For the best long-term health, practice body condition scoring, use the growth charts, and try not to over- or underfeed. Refrigerate, or freeze the remainder.

See Chapt. 5 for growth charts and portion sizing, Chapt. 6 for substitutions, Chapts. 8-10 for additional method details, tips, & advice, Chapt. 11 for storage info. and Chapt. 12 for online suppliers.

Nutritional Information

MACRONUTRIENT ANALYSIS			
Composition	As formulated	Dry Matter	% kcal
Protein	18%	55%	46%
Fat	8%	25%	50%
Ash	3%	9%	
Moisture	67%		
Fiber	2%	7%	
Net Carbs	2%	5%	4%
Sugars	1%	2%	1%
Starch	3%	8%	7%
Total			100%

MACRONUTRIENT INFORMATION				
Total kcal in recipe				10000
kcal / oz				39
kcal / lb				617
kcal / 100g				136
kcal / kg				1,360

MINERALS				
	Unit	Min	Max	Recipe
Ca	g	2.5	4	3.64
P	g	2.25		3.35
Ca:P	ratio	1:1	1.8:1	1.09 : 1
K	g	1.1		3.18
Na	g	0.55		0.78
MG	g	0.1		0.43
Cl	g	0.83		0.98
Fe	mg	22	350	22.43
Cu	mg	2.75	7	3.61
Mn	mg	1.4	40	5.53
Zn	mg	25	70	39.99
I	mg	0.38	3	0.38
Se	mg	0.1		0.24

VITAMINS				
	Unit	Min	Max	Recipe
Vit A	IU	1,250		1457.2
Vit C	mg			103.96
Vit D	IU	138		1520.73
Vit E	IU	12.5		17.19
Thiamine, B1	mg	0.45		0.98
Riboflavine, B2	mg	1.05		1.4
Niacin, B3	mg	3.4		43.79
Pantothenic Acid, B5	mg	3		6.29
B6 (Pyridoxine)	mg	0.3		2.94
Vit B12	mg	0.01		0.03
Folic Acid	mg	0.05		0.21
Choline	mg	425		463.81
Vit K1	mg			0.02
Biotin	mg			0.44

FATS				
	Unit	Min	Max	Recipe
Total	g	21.25		58.6
Saturated	g			10.3
Monounsaturated	g			21.88
Polyunsaturated	g			17.79
LA	g	3.25	16.25	5.3
ALA	g	0.2		4.61
AA	g	0.08		0.33
EPA	g			2.13
DPA	g			0.47
DHA	g			3.24
Omega-6/Omega-3	ratio			0.55 : 1
EPA + DHA	g	0.13		5.37

AMINO ACIDS				
	Unit	Min	Max	Recipe
Total protein	g	62.5		130.82
Tryptophan	g	0.58		1.5
Threonine	g	2.03		5.55
Isoleucine	g	1.63		5.92
Leucine	g	3.23		10.12
Lysine*	g	2.2	7*	10.92
Methionine	g	0.88		3.57
M - Cystine	g	1.75		5.05
Phenylalanine	g	1.63		5.26
P - Tyrosine	g	3.25		9.9
Valine	g	1.7		6.72
Arginine	g	2.05		8.4
Histidine	g	0.98		3.52
Purines	mg			790.67
Taurine	g			0.34

Zeva's Fruity Fish

& Brocolli

Fish is particularly gentle on puppy tummies, and I have yet to meet a dog of any age who doesn't go potty for oysters! Check out Chapter 12 for online suppliers if you struggle to obtain oysters.

Formulated to FEDIAF

Ingredients

3,347g Whitefish

    3,347g Oily fish

    542g Oysters

    190g Beef liver

    781g Broccoli

    279g Apples

    245g Brazil nuts

    153g Turmeric

    115g Bonemeal

    85g Spirulina

    5g Kelp (I = 700mcg/g)

Please weigh all ingredients accurately.

To thoroughly mix the recipe, you will need a large mixing bowl, tub, or small bucket and a large, sturdy, long-handled spoon.

Method

1. Pull the heads off the fish and keep them whole or cut into bite-sized chunks to match the size of your puppy. Place in your mixing bowl.

2. Chop about half the fish into bite-sized chunks and grind the rest with the oysters and liver. Put everything in the bowl.

3. Roughly chop the broccoli and apples and put them through a juicer. Add both juice and pulp into the mix. If you

don't have a juicer, finely chop the broccoli florets and grate the stems with the apples.

4. Chop the Brazil nuts.

5. Now add all the dry powdered ingredients: turmeric, bonemeal, spirulina, & kelp.

6. Weigh out a suitably sized portion to serve to your puppy, who has no doubt been supervising proceedings.

For the best long-term health, practice body condition scoring, use the growth charts, and try not to over- or underfeed. Refrigerate or freeze the remainder.

See Chapt. 5 for growth charts and portion sizing, Chapt. 6 for substitutions, Chapts. 8-10 for additional method details, tips, & advice, Chapt. 11 for storage info. and Chapt. 12 for online suppliers.

Nutritional Information

MACRONUTRIENT ANALYSIS			
Composition	As formulated	Dry Matter	% kcal
Protein	17%	61%	53.41%
Fat	5%	19%	41.10%
Ash	3%	9%	
Moisture	73%		
Fiber	1%	4%	
Net Carbs	2%	6%	5.49%
Sugars	1%	3%	2.20%
Starch	1%	5%	4.27%
Total			100%

MACRONUTRIENT INFORMATION	
Total kcal in recipe	10,000
kcal / oz	31.2
kcal / lb	499
kcal / 100g	110
kcal / kg	1,100

MINERALS				
	Unit	Min	Max	Recipe
Ca	g	2.5	4	3.98
P	g	2.25		3.54
Ca:P	ratio	1:1	1.8:1	1.12:1
K	g	1.1		3.33
Na	g	0.55		0.89
MG	g	0.1		0.41
Cl	g	0.83		1.27
Fe	mg	22	350	23.4
Cu	mg	2.75	7	4.74
Mn	mg	1.4	40	4.26
Zn	mg	25	70	26.76
I	mg	0.38	3	0.55
Se	mg	0.1		0.72

FATS				
	Unit	Min	Max	Recipe
Total	g	21.25		48.36
Saturated	g			11.43
Monounsaturated	g			16.24
Polyunsaturated	g			13.51
LA	g	3.25	16.25	5.71
ALA	g	0.2		0.45
AA	g	0.08		0.41
EPA	g			1.97
DPA	g			0.34
DHA	g			3.61
Omega-6/Omega-3	ratio			1.05:1
EPA + DHA	g	0.13		5.58

FATS				
	Unit	Min	Max	Recipe
Total	g	21.25		48.36
Saturated	g			11.43
Monounsaturated	g			16.24
Polyunsaturated	g			13.51
LA	g	3.25	16.25	5.71
ALA	g	0.2		0.45
AA	g	0.08		0.41
EPA	g			1.97
DPA	g			0.34
DHA	g			3.61
Omega-6/Omega-3	ratio			1.05 : 1
EPA + DHA	g	0.13		5.58

AMINO ACIDS				
	Unit	Min	Max	Recipe
Total protein	g	62.5		152.6
Tryptophan	g	0.58		1.74
Threonine	g	2.03		6.49
Isoleucine	g	1.63		6.98
Leucine	g	3.23		12.18
Lysine*	g	2.2	7*	13.18
Methionine	g	0.88		4.46
M - Cystine	g	1.75		6.16
Phenylalanine	g	1.63		6.05
P - Tyrosine	g	3.25		11.25
Valine	g	1.7		7.85
Arginine	g	2.05		9.61
Histidine	g	0.98		4.15
Purines	mg			1309.91
Taurine	g			0.84

Nimue's Chicken

& Brussels

Nimue is 10 years old now. Our vet commented at her annual checkup that she appears every bit like a dog half her age. Is it those Brussels, I wonder? Although far from being a pup, this is still one of her favorite recipes. If you don't have any oysters, you can add 120mg of zinc and increase the amount of copper to 14mg. The total recipe kcals would drop to 9,770.

Formulated to FEDIAF

Ingredients

4,318g Chicken, no skin or bone

1,107g Chicken gizzards

922g Chicken legs incl. skin and bone

830g Chicken liver

738g Chicken hearts

333g Oysters

1,199g Brussels sprouts

115g Flax or chia seeds

65g Bonemeal

26g Turmeric powder

17g Salt

12g Kelp powder (I = 700mcg/g)

8mg Copper, e.g. 4 capsules at 2 mg/cap

16g Cod liver oil

Please weigh all ingredients accurately.

This recipe requires a meat grinder/mincer that is able to cope with poultry bones.

You will need a large mixing bowl, tub, or small bucket and a large, sturdy, long-handled spoon to thoroughly mix the recipe.

Method

1. Chop roughly half of the chicken meat into bite-sized chunks and place in the bowl.

2. Grind together the remaining chicken and chicken legs, including skin and bone, liver, hearts, and oysters, and add them to the bowl.

3. Run the Brussels through a juicer and add both juice and pulp to the bowl. Or chop finely.

4. Grind the seeds before adding them to the mix

5. Now add all the dry powdered ingredients: bonemeal, turmeric, salt & kelp

6. Twist open any supplement capsules and sprinkle the powder into the bowl

7. Roughly mix everything until no dry powders are visible

8. Add the cod liver oil, then thoroughly mix the entire recipe

9. Weigh out a suitably sized portion and serve

For the best long-term health, practice body condition scoring, use the growth charts, and try not to over- or underfeed. Refrigerate or freeze the remainder.

See Chapt. 5 for growth charts and portion sizing, Chapt. 6 for substitutions, Chapts. 8-10 for additional method details, tips, & advice, Chapt. 11 for storage info. and Chapt. 12 for online suppliers.

Nutritional Information

MACRONUTRIENT ANALYSIS			
Composition	As formulated	Dry Matter	% kcal
Protein	18%	67%	60%
Fat	4%	17%	37%
Ash	2%	8%	
Moisture	74%		
Fiber	1%	3%	
Net Carbs	1%	4%	4%
Sugars	0%	1%	1%
Starch	0%	2%	2%
Total			100%

MACRONUTRIENT INFORMATION				
Total kcal in recipe				10,000
kcal / oz				29
kcal / lb				467
kcal / 100g				103
kcal / kg				1030

MINERALS				
	Unit	Min	Max	Recipe
Ca	g	2.5	4	3.17
P	g	2.25		3.17
Ca:P	ratio	1:1	1.8:1	1.00 : 1
K	g	1.1		2.68
Na	g	0.55		1.29
MG	g	0.1		0.32
Cl	g	0.83		1.59
Fe	mg	22	350	25.07
Cu	mg	2.75	7	3.58
Mn	mg	1.4	40	1.85
Zn	mg	25	70	25.09
I	mg	0.38	3	0.85
Se	mg	0.1		0.22

VITAMINS				
	Unit	Min	Max	Recipe
Vit A	IU	1,250		18122.21
Vit C	mg			133.52
Vit D	IU	138		263.64
Vit E	IU	12.5		14.09
Thiamine, B1	mg	0.45		1.26
Riboflavine, B2	mg	1.05		3.52
Niacin, B3	mg	3.4		68.37
Pantothenic Acid, B5	mg	3		13.74
B6 (Pyridoxine)	mg	0.3		4.18
Vit B12	mg	0.01		0.04
Folic Acid	mg	0.05		0.67
Choline	mg	425		793.99
Vit K1	mg			0.23
Biotin	mg			1.07

FATS				
	Unit	Min	Max	Recipe
Total	g	21.25		43.28
Saturated	g			10.86
Monounsaturated	g			12.73
Polyunsaturated	g			12.28
LA	g	3.25	16.25	6.27
ALA	g	0.2		2.58
AA	g	0.08		1.41
EPA	g			0.27
DPA	g			0.11
DHA	g			0.43
Omega-6/Omega-3	ratio			2.15 : 1
EPA + DHA	g	0.13		0.7

AMINO ACIDS				
	Unit	Min	Max	Recipe
Total protein	g	62.5		170.53
Tryptophan	g	0.58		1.99
Threonine	g	2.03		7.33
Isoleucine	g	1.63		8.6
Leucine	g	3.23		13.03
Lysine*	g	2.2	7*	14.12
Methionine	g	0.88		4.47
M - Cystine	g	1.75		6.65
Phenylalanine	g	1.63		7.03
P - Tyrosine	g	3.25		12.67
Valine	g	1.7		8.63
Arginine	g	2.05		10.92
Histidine	g	0.98		5.12
Purines	mg			1431.21
Taurine	g			0.42

COOKED or RAW.

Puppies under 50% of their anticipated adult weight

Likely 14 weeks old and younger. Cooking is optional. These recipes have all been formulated and nutritionally balanced based on whether they are eaten raw or cooked. See Chapter 8 for more details about cooking methods.

The puppy weight for these recipes is less than 50% of their final anticipated adult weight. This likely means your puppy is under 14 weeks old. See Chapter 5 for more information about different growth phases, growth charts, and how to score body condition.

Although values for kcals per recipe weight are provided, these will vary according to the final finished recipe weight, which varies according to water content after cooking. To calculate more accurate values if you cook a recipe, please see Chapter 11.

In all recipes that might be cooked, we do not include natural sources of bone such as poultry wings, necks, and backs because cooked poultry bone can lead to sharp shards with potential internal injury or obstruction risks.

Baxter's Beef
& Egg

Baxter was my father's dog when he was a young man. They lived on the edge of an industrial steel town and walked in farmland on the weekend. When he got paid, Dad would go buy beef from the farmer, and although he had to deliver most of it to his mother, he always kept some back for Baxter.

Formulated to AAFCO

Ingredients

2,584g Beef, ground, 90% lean

1,938 Beef Tripe

258 Beef Spleen

258g Beef Liver, freeze-dried

388g Eggs, no shell

646g Green leafy veg. mix

269g Hemp seed

86g Bonemeal

26g Ginger powder

18g Salt

7g Kelp powder (I =700 mcg/g)

30mg Zinc, e.g. 2 capsules at 15 mg/cap

32g Cod liver oil

Please weigh all ingredients accurately.

You will need a large mixing bowl, tub, or small bucket and a large, sturdy, long-handled spoon to thoroughly mix the recipe.

Method – cooking is optional.

1. Place the ground beef into the mixing bowl.

2. If the tripe is not ground, then cut it into bite-sized chunks and add to the bowl.

3. Chop the spleen finely to aid even distribution and add to the bowl

4. Chop the liver if necessary, but leave it in chunks to add a chewy texture

5. Crack the eggs directly into the mix

6. Chop the leafy greens and add to the bowl

7. Mix.

8. If you plan to cook, divide the mixture into manageable portions to slow roast in single or multiple crock pots or roasting pans. Leave the lids on or wrap well to reduce moisture loss and slow cook at 212F/100C for 3 to 4 hours.

9. Once cooked, allow to cool. Using your hands, crumble the meat back into the mixing bowl.

10. Grind the hemp seed and add it to the bowl

11. Now add all the dry powdered ingredients: bonemeal, ginger, salt & kelp

12. Roughly mix everything until no dry powders are visible

13. Add the cod liver oil, then thoroughly mix the entire recipe

14. Weigh out a suitably sized portion to serve to your puppy. Ensure you wipe any dog drool from the floor, because it is very slippery!

For the best long-term health, practice body condition scoring, use the growth charts, and try not to over- or underfeed. Refrigerate or freeze the remainder.

See Chapt. 5 for growth charts and portion sizing, Chapt. 6 for substitutions, Chapts. 8-10 for additional method details, tips, & advice, Chapt. 11 for storage info. and Chapt. 12 for online suppliers.

Nutritional Information

MACRONUTRIENT ANALYSIS			
Composition	As formulated	Dry Matter	% kcal
Protein	20%	61%	51%
Fat	8%	25%	47%
Ash	3%	9%	
Moisture	67%		
Fiber	1%	2%	
Net Carbs	1%	3%	2%
Sugars	1%	2%	2%
Starch	0%	0%	0%
Total			100%

MACRONUTRIENT INFORMATION	
Total kcal in recipe	10,000
kcal / oz	45
kcal / lb	715
kcal / 100g	110
kcal / kg	1,098

MINERALS				
	Unit	Min	Max	Recipe
Ca	g	3	4.5	3
P	g	2.5	4	2.79
Ca:P	ratio	01:01	2.1	1.08 : 1
K	g	1.5		2.21
Na	g	0.8		1.24
MG	g	0.15		0.36
Cl	g	1.1		1.22
Fe	mg	22		27.7
Cu	mg	3.1		9.53
Mn	mg	1.8		2.91
Zn	mg	25		26.03
I	mg	0.25	2.75	0.43
Se	mg	0.09		0.15

VITAMINS				
	Unit	Min	Max	Recipe
Vit A	IU	1,250	62,500	12492.77
Vit C	mg			21.95
Vit D	IU	125	750	486.37
Vit E	IU	12.5		12.5
Thiamine, B1	mg	0.56		0.58
Riboflavine, B2	mg	1.3		3.36
Niacin, B3	mg	3.4		32.37
Pantothenic Acid, B5	mg	3		8.35
B6 (Pyridoxine)	mg	0.38		1.44
Vit B12	mg	0.01		0.04
Folic Acid	mg	0.05		0.22
Choline	mg	340		463.71
Vit K1	mg			0.2
Biotin	mg			0.09

FATS				
	Unit	Min	Max	Recipe
Total	g	21.3		51.97
Saturated	g			16.08
Monounsaturated	g			17.32
Polyunsaturated	g			12.62
LA	g	3.3		8.5
ALA	g	0.2		2.07
AA	g	0.08		0.37
EPA	g			0.27
DPA	g			0.04
DHA	g			0.34
Omega-6/Omega-3	ratio		30:1	3.05 : 1
EPA + DHA	g	0.1		0.62

AMINO ACIDS				
	Unit	Min	Max	Recipe
Total protein	g	56.3		127.44
Tryptophan	g	0.5		1.04
Threonine	g	2.6		4.58
Isoleucine	g	1.78		4.67
Leucine	g	3.23		9.2
Lysine*	g	2.25		9.57
Methionine	g	0.88		3.04
M - Cystine	g	1.75		4.5
Phenylalanine	g	2.08		4.66
P - Tyrosine	g	3.25		7.77
Valine	g	1.7		5.46
Arginine	g	2.5		7.24
Histidine	g	1.1		3.55
Purines	mg	0		508.8
Taurine	g	0		0.64

NB kcal per weight values will vary according to cooking or if raw. The values given are based on cooked as per the recipe.

Lola's Lamb

& Mushrooms

Lola was a puppy from our first-ever litter, a real character through and through. She was always first in the bowl for a lamb dinner. We often leave small fish heads whole for puppies to chew on. Lola would dig about, pick one out, and run off to eat it in peace, away from the other puppies!

Formulated to FEDIAF

Ingredients

3,418g Lamb, 85% lean

342g Lamb heart

273g Beef liver

855g Herring

298g Oysters

513g Mushrooms

342g Eggs, no shell

342g Kale

103g Turmeric powder

92g Parsley

85g Bonemeal

10g Salt

6g Kelp powder (I = 700mcg/g)

1,400mg Choline e.g 4 capsules at 350mg/cap

36mg Iron e.g. 2 capsules at 18mg/cap

23g Cod liver oil

Please weigh all ingredients accurately.

You will need a large mixing bowl, tub or small bucket and a large, sturdy, long-handled spoon to thoroughly mix the recipe.

Method – Cooking is optional

1. Chop about half the lamb into bite-sized chunks to suit your puppy's size and place in a large mixing bowl.

2. Twist off the herring heads and put them in the bowl as a chewy treat.

3. Grind the rest of the lamb, herrings, heart, liver, and oysters together and add them to the bowl.

4. Crack the eggs straight into the bowl.

5. If you plan to cook, divide the mixture into manageable portions to slow roast in single or multiple crock pots or roasting pans. Leave the lids on or wrap well to reduce moisture loss and slow cook at 212F/100C for 3 to 4 hours.

6. Once cooked, allow to cool. Using your hands, crumble the meat back into the mixing bowl.

7. Finely chop the kale or put it through a juicer and add the juice and pulp to the bowl.

8. Even if you keep the rest raw, chop and lightly cook the mushrooms. Add to the mix.

9. Now add all the dry powdered ingredients: turmeric, parsley, bonemeal, salt & kelp.

10. Twist open any supplement capsules and sprinkle the powder into the bowl

11. Roughly mix everything until no dry powders are visible

12. Add the cod liver oil, then thoroughly mix the entire recipe

13. Weigh out a suitably sized portion to serve to your puppy.

For the best long-term health, practice body condition scoring, use the growth charts, and try not to over- or underfeed. Refrigerate or freeze the remainder.

See Chapt. 5 for growth charts and portion sizing, Chapt. 6 for substitutions, Chapts. 8-10 for additional method details, tips, & advice, Chapt. 11 for storage info. and Chapt. 12 for online suppliers.

Nutritional Information

MACRONUTRIENT ANALYSIS			
Composition	As formulated	Dry Matter	% kcal
Protein	16%	49%	37%
Fat	10%	33%	59%
Ash	3%	8%	
Moisture	69%		
Fiber	1%	4%	
Net Carbs	2%	6%	4%
Sugars	1%	2%	1%
Starch	1%	3%	2%
Total			100%

MACRONUTRIENT INFORMATION	
Total kcal in recipe	10,000
kcal / oz	42
kcal / lb	677
kcal / 100g	149
kcal / kg	1,491

MINERALS				
	Unit	Min	Max	Recipe
Ca	g	2.5	4	3
P	g	2.25		2.41
Ca:P	ratio	1:1	1.8:1	1.25:1
K	g	1.1		2.21
Na	g	0.55		0.87
MG	g	0.1		0.21
Cl	g	0.83		0.92
Fe	mg	22	350	22.86
Cu	mg	2.75	7	4.4
Mn	mg	1.4	40	3.56
Zn	mg	25	70	26.32
I	mg	0.38	3	0.45
Se	mg	0.1		0.16

VITAMINS				
	Unit	Min	Max	Recipe
Vit A	IU	1,250		5627.2
Vit C	mg			16.12
Vit D	IU	138		468.51
Vit E	IU	12.5		13.13
Thiamine, B1	mg	0.45		0.47
Riboflavine, B2	mg	1.05		2.42
Niacin, B3	mg	3.4		33.43
Pantothenic Acid, B5	mg	3		6.79
B6 (Pyridoxine)	mg	0.3		0.79
Vit B12	mg	0.01		0.03
Folic Acid	mg	0.05		0.18
Choline	mg	425		471.23
Vit K1	mg			0.13
Biotin	mg			0.37

FATS				
	Unit	Min	Max	Recipe
Total	g	21.25		69.55
Saturated	g			28.07
Monounsaturated	g			25.19
Polyunsaturated	g			7.99
LA	g	3.25	16.25	4.08
ALA	g	0.2		0.93
AA	g	0.08		0.33
EPA	g			0.97
DPA	g			0.16
DHA	g			1.06
Omega-6/Omega-3	ratio			1.48 : 1
EPA + DHA	g	0.13		2.03

AMINO ACIDS				
	Unit	Min	Max	Recipe
Total protein	g	62.5		104.44
Tryptophan	g	0.58		1.18
Threonine	g	2.03		4.49
Isoleucine	g	1.63		4.64
Leucine	g	3.23		8.01
Lysine*	g	2.2	7*	8.73
Methionine	g	0.88		2.69
M - Cystine	g	1.75		3.86
Phenylalanine	g	1.63		4.32
P - Tyrosine	g	3.25		7.84
Valine	g	1.7		5.15
Arginine	g	2.05		6.12
Histidine	g	0.98		2.84
Purines	mg			519.44
Taurine	g			0.13

NB kcal per weight values will vary according to cooking or if raw. The values given are based on cooked as per the recipe.

Pablo's Chicken

& Carrots

Oysters are an excellent source of zinc, and puppies adore them. We bulk buy canned and finish off opened cans for lunch on toasted wholewheat bread, yum. In this recipe, if you don't have any oysters, you can replace them with 135mg zinc supplement (typically 9 capsules at 15mg/cap) but also increase the beef liver to 220g, turmeric to 200g, and salt to 20g to replace the copper, iron & chloride from the oysters. Total recipe kcal will reduce to 9,888.

Formulated to AAFCO

Ingredients

3,202g Chicken thigh meat (no bone or skin)

1427g Chicken breast meat (no bone or skin)

216g Beef liver, fresh

100g Chicken liver, fresh

600g Sardines, canned or fresh

366 Oysters, canned or fresh

800g Carrots

125g Pumpkin seeds

196g Turmeric powder

105g Bonemeal

59g Parsley, dried

20g Salt, finely ground

5g Nutritional yeast

5g Kelp powder

28g Cod liver oil

Please weigh all ingredients accurately.

You will need a large mixing bowl, tub, or small bucket and a large, sturdy, long-handled spoon to thoroughly mix the recipe.

Method – Cooking is optional

1. Steam the chicken until tender, then chop approximately half into bite-sized chunks and grind the rest. Place in a large mixing bowl.

2. Steam the livers, grind them, and add them to the bowl

3. If the sardines & oysters are fresh, steam them before mincing and adding to the mix.

4. Slice the carrots, then steam or simmer until just tender. These can be added directly to the mixing bowl, although we usually mash for puppies at this age so they are not tempted to pick bits out to leave behind. If raw, preferably juice the carrots and add both juice and pulp to mix. Or grate them if you have no juicer.

5. Grind pumpkin seeds and add to bowl.

6. Add dry ingredients: turmeric, bonemeal, parsley, salt, yeast, and kelp.

7. Roughly mix the recipe so that no dry powders remain visible

8. Add the cod liver oil and thoroughly mix everything together

9. Weigh out a suitably sized portion to serve to your puppy.

For the best long-term health, practice body condition scoring, use the growth charts, and try not to over- or underfeed. Refrigerate or freeze the remainder.

See Chapt. 5 for growth charts and portion sizing, Chapt. 6 for substitutions, Chapts. 8-10 for additional method details, tips, & advice, Chapt. 11 for storage info. and Chapt. 12 for online suppliers.

Nutritional Information

MACRONUTRIENT ANALYSIS			
Composition	As formulated	Dry Matter	% kcal
Protein	21%	62%	54%
Fat	7%	20%	42%
Ash	3%	9%	
Moisture	66%		
Fiber	1%	3%	
Net Carbs	2%	5%	4%
Sugars	1%	2%	2%
Starch	1%	4%	3%
Total			100%

MACRONUTRIENT INFORMATION				
Total kcal in recipe				10,000
kcal / oz				39
kcal / lb				628
kcal / 100g				138
kcal / kg				1384

MINERALS				
	Unit	Min	Max	Recipe
Ca	g	3	4.5	3.08
P	g	2.5	4	2.63
Ca:P	ratio	01:01	2.1	1.17 : 1
K	g	1.5		2.34
Na	g	0.8		1.48
MG	g	0.15		0.3
Cl	g	1.1		1.27
Fe	mg	22		23.8
Cu	mg	3.1		4.02
Mn	mg	1.8		5.07
Zn	mg	25		38.2
I	mg	0.25	2.75	2.41
Se	mg	0.09		0.19

VITAMINS				
	Unit	Min	Max	Recipe
Vit A	IU	1,250	62,500	15772.82
Vit C	mg			9.54
Vit D	IU	125	750	485.69
Vit E	IU	12.5		12.52
Thiamine, B1	mg	0.56		0.59
Riboflavine, B2	mg	1.3		2.18
Niacin, B3	mg	3.4		44.98
Pantothenic Acid, B5	mg	3		8
B6 (Pyridoxine)	mg	0.38		1.58
Vit B12	mg	0.01		0.02
Folic Acid	mg	0.05		0.15
Choline	mg	340		383.05
Vit K1	mg			0.1
Biotin	mg			0.25

FATS				
	Unit	Min	Max	Recipe
Total	g	21.3		49.44
Saturated	g			13.38
Monounsaturated	g			19.28
Polyunsaturated	g			11.81
LA	g	3.3		8.09
ALA	g	0.2		0.43
AA	g	0.08		0.68
EPA	g			0.71
DPA	g			0.11
DHA	g			0.93
Omega-6/Omega-3	ratio		30:1	4.28 : 1
EPA + DHA	g	0.1		1.64

AMINO ACIDS				
	Unit	Min	Max	Recipe
Total protein	g	56.3		152.85
Tryptophan	g	0.5		1.74
Threonine	g	2.6		6.78
Isoleucine	g	1.78		7.38
Leucine	g	3.23		12.28
Lysine*	g	2.25		13.16
Methionine	g	0.88		4.14
M - Cystine	g	1.75		6.01
Phenylalanine	g	2.08		6.23
P - Tyrosine	g	3.25		11.7
Valine	g	1.7		7.54
Arginine	g	2.5		10.31
Histidine	g	1.1		4.57
Purines	mg	0		114.14
Taurine	g	0		0.12

NB kcal per weight values will vary according to cooking or if raw. The values given are based on cooked as per the recipe.

Magick's Mixed Meat Medley

With Brocolli

Magick is perhaps the most unique puppy we have enjoyed raising. She was the most inquisitive and independent of her litter. She was always into everything and always doing things her own way. Clearly hugely intelligent and a real thinker. Fortunately, we had exactly the right personality owner to make the most of her amazing talents, and she is loving life as a specialist demonstration dog with a huge personality! You can meet her at www.extra.dog

Formulated to FEDIAF

2,423 Beef Tripe

1,743 Lamb, 85% lean

953g Sardines or other oily fish

872g Chicken breast meat, no skin

364g Lamb Heart

290g Lamb kidney

120g Lamb liver

1,143g Broccoli

421g Oysters

117g Spirulina powder

69g Bonemeal

45g Turmeric powder

8g Salt

7g Kelp powder

3g Nutritional yeast

37g Cod liver oil

10g Sunflower or Safflower oil

Please weigh all ingredients accurately. Cooking is optional.

You will need a large mixing bowl, tub, or small bucket and a large, sturdy, long-handled spoon to thoroughly mix the recipe.

Method – cooking is optional

1. Steam the tripe if you must, but open your windows first!

2. Tightly wrap the lamb and set it to slow roast while you combine the rest of the recipe.

3. Steam the sardines, chicken breast, and lamb offals, then grind them together.

4. Steam the broccoli, but if you are not cooking this recipe, chop the florets and grate the stem, or preferably put it through a juicer. Then, add both the juice and pulp to the mixing bowl.

5. Add the oysters to the bowl.

6. Once the lamb is ready, shred it straight into the bowl. If you keep it raw, chop half into bite-sized chunks and grind the rest.

7. Now add all your dry powder ingredients: spirulina, bonemeal, turmeric, salt, kelp, and yeast.

8. Roughly mix until no dry powders remain visible

9. Add the oils and thoroughly mix the whole recipe together.

10. Weigh out a suitably sized portion to serve to your puppy. Dinner is served.

For the best long-term health, practice body condition scoring, use the growth charts, and try not to over- or underfeed. Refrigerate or freeze the remainder.

See Chapt. 5 for growth charts and portion sizing, Chapt. 6 for substitutions, Chapts. 8-10 for additional method details, tips, & advice, Chapt. 11 for storage info. and Chapt. 12 for online suppliers.

Nutritional Information

MACRONUTRIENT ANALYSIS			
Composition	As formulated	Dry Matter	% kcal
Protein	15%	59%	47%
Fat	7%	26%	49%
Ash	2%	8%	
Moisture	74%		
Fiber	1%	2%	
Net Carbs	1%	5%	4%
Sugars	0%	1%	1%
Starch	1%	2%	2%
Total			100%

MACRONUTRIENT INFORMATION					
Total kcal in recipe					10,000
kcal / oz					33
kcal / lb					526
kcal / 100g					116
kcal / kg					1,159

MINERALS				
	Unit	Min	Max	Recipe
Ca	g	2.5	4	2.72
P	g	2.25		2.46
Ca:P	ratio	1:1	1.8:1	1.11 : 1
K	g	1.1		2.27
Na	g	0.55		1.16
MG	g	0.1		0.23
Cl	g	0.83		1.13
Fe	mg	22	350	27.88
Cu	mg	2.75	7	3.64
Mn	mg	1.4	40	2.13
Zn	mg	25	70	29.84
I	mg	0.38	3	0.5
Se	mg	0.1		0.21

VITAMINS				
	Unit	Min	Max	Recipe
Vit A	IU	1,250		4925.23
Vit C	mg			81.7
Vit D	IU	138		636.76
Vit E	IU	12.5		16.5
Thiamine, B1	mg	0.45		0.77
Riboflavine, B2	mg	1.05		2.86
Niacin, B3	mg	3.4		34
Pantothenic Acid, B5	mg	3		6.71
B6 (Pyridoxine)	mg	0.3		0.83
Vit B12	mg	0.01		0.03
Folic Acid	mg	0.05		0.17
Choline	mg	425		634.17
Vit K1	mg			0.1
Biotin	mg			0.19

FATS				
	Unit	Min	Max	Recipe
Total	g	21.25		57.93
Saturated	g			21.47
Monounsaturated	g			21.38
Polyunsaturated	g			7.91
LA	g	3.25	16.25	3.29
ALA	g	0.2		0.94
AA	g	0.08		0.66
EPA	g			1.06
DPA	g			0.22
DHA	g			1.35
Omega-6/Omega-3	ratio			1.17 : 1
EPA + DHA	g	0.13		2.41

AMINO ACIDS				
	Unit	Min	Max	Recipe
Total protein	g	62.5		133.08
Tryptophan	g	0.58		1.44
Threonine	g	2.03		5.44
Isoleucine	g	1.63		5.87
Leucine	g	3.23		9.88
Lysine*	g	2.2	7*	10.39
Methionine	g	0.88		3.53
M - Cystine	g	1.75		4.94
Phenylalanine	g	1.63		5.35
P - Tyrosine	g	3.25		9.82
Valine	g	1.7		6.37
Arginine	g	2.05		8.11
Histidine	g	0.98		3.95
Purines	mg			950.48
Taurine	g			0.26

NB kcal per weight values will vary according to cooking or if raw. The values given are based on cooked as per the recipe.

Buddy's Lamb

& Egg

Every litter of puppies has a dominant, bossy pup, and Buddy was most certainly that pup in his litter! He even used to take on his mother and try to tell her his opinion, but she only stood for so much before putting him in his place. He grew up to be the most beautiful, loving boy and dotes upon his step-sister, who came along two years later. He learned to be a gentleman, after all!

Formulated to FEDIAF

Ingredients

3,218g Lamb, 85% lean

503g Whole egg, no shell

503g Beef heart

404g Beef liver

194g Beef spleen

274g Oysters

160g Hemp seed

123g Poppy seed

77g Bonemeal

10g Salt

7g Kelp powder (I = 700mcg/g)

28g Cod liver oil

Please take care to weigh all ingredients accurately.

You will need a large mixing bowl, tub or small bucket and a large, sturdy, long-handled spoon to thoroughly mix the recipe.

Method – Cooking is optional

1. Chop roughly half the lamb into bite-sized chunks and add to the bowl

2. Grind the remaining lamb along with the heart, liver, spleen & oysters

3. Crack the eggs straight into the bowl and mix everything

4. Divide the mixture in order to fit into 1 or multiple roasting tins, crock pots or casserole dishes and slow cook in the oven at 212F/100C for around 3 to 4 hours.

5. Once the meat mix is cooked, allow to cool and then use your hands to crumble the mix back into the bowl

6. Grind and add the hemp and poppy seeds

7. Now add the dry powdered ingredients; bonemeal, salt & kelp

8. Roughly mix everything until no dry powders are visible

9. Add the cod liver oil then thoroughly mix the entire recipe

10. Weigh out a suitably sized portion to serve to your puppy.

Practice body condition scoring, use the growth charts and try not to over or under-feed for the best long-term health. Refrigerate, or freeze the remainder.

See Chapt. 5 for growth charts and portion sizing, Chapt. 6 for substitutions, Chapts. 8-10 for additional method details, tips, & advice, Chapt. 11 for storage info. and Chapt. 12 for online suppliers.

Nutritional Information

MACRONUTRIENT ANALYSIS			
Composition	As formulated	Dry Matter	% kcal
Protein	18%	50%	35%
Fat	13%	37%	63%
Ash	3%	8%	
Moisture	64%		
Fiber	1%	2%	
Net Carbs	1%	3%	2%
Sugars	1%	2%	1%
Starch	0%	1%	1%
Total			100%

MACRONUTRIENT INFORMATION				
Total kcal in recipe				10,000
kcal / oz				52
kcal / lb				825
kcal / 100g				182
kcal / kg				1,818

MINERALS				
	Unit	Min	Max	Recipe
Ca	g	2.5	4	2.66
P	g	2.25		2.45
Ca:P	ratio	1:1	1.8:1	1.09 : 1
K	g	1.1		1.51
Na	g	0.55		0.8
MG	g	0.1		0.26
Cl	g	0.83		0.97
Fe	mg	22	350	21.89
Cu	mg	2.75	7	5.82
Mn	mg	1.4	40	2.44
Zn	mg	25	70	26.59
I	mg	0.38	3	0.47
Se	mg	0.1		0.14

VITAMINS				
	Unit	Min	Max	Recipe
Vit A	IU	1,250		5983.17
Vit C	mg			11.13
Vit D	IU	138		433.69
Vit E	IU	12.5		12.52
Thiamine, B1	mg	0.45		0.56
Riboflavine, B2	mg	1.05		2.42
Niacin, B3	mg	3.4		31.66
Pantothenic Acid, B5	mg	3		6.78
B6 (Pyridoxine)	mg	0.3		0.66
Vit B12	mg	0.01		0.03
Folic Acid	mg	0.05		0.17
Choline	mg	425		433.84
Vit K1	mg			0.01
Biotin	mg			0.5

FATS				
	Unit	Min	Max	Recipe
Total	g	21.25		74.05
Saturated	g			27.38
Monounsaturated	g			23.63
Polyunsaturated	g			15.47
LA	g	3.25	16.25	11.45
ALA	g	0.2		2.12
AA	g	0.08		0.34
EPA	g			0.38
DPA	g			0.11
DHA	g			0.37
Omega-6/Omega-3	ratio			3.83 : 1
EPA + DHA	g	0.13		0.74

AMINO ACIDS				
	Unit	Min	Max	Recipe
Total protein	g	62.5		99.69
Tryptophan	g	0.58		1.15
Threonine	g	2.03		4.28
Isoleucine	g	1.63		4.49
Leucine	g	3.23		7.85
Lysine*	g	2.2	7*	8.17
Methionine	g	0.88		2.72
M - Cystine	g	1.75		4.06
Phenylalanine	g	1.63		4.31
P - Tyrosine	g	3.25		7.87
Valine	g	1.7		5.16
Arginine	g	2.05		6.61
Histidine	g	0.98		2.95
Purines	mg			519.69
Taurine	g			0.15

NB kcal per weight values will vary according to cooking or if raw. The values given are based on cooked as per the recipe.

LOW PURINE. Puppies under 50% of their anticipated adult weight

Likely 14 weeks old and younger

These balanced, low-purine recipes are suitable for Dalmatians (HUA) and other puppies with hyperuricosuria. They are also entirely suitable and balanced for other puppies, but puppies (and adult dogs) with hyperuricosuria must ONLY be fed from the low-purine recipe ranges in each section.

They include a range of raw and cooked options. By necessity, these contain more supplementation as the necessary nutrient balance for puppies cannot readily be achieved solely through whole foods with no secreting organ meat, oily fish, oysters, or other high purine ingredients. As a result, they tend to be simpler recipes with fewer ingredients and can, therefore, be easier for people who struggle to source offals. They are still predominantly healthy, homemade, unprocessed whole-food recipes.

If you have a Dalmatian, they WILL have Hyperuricosuria (unless you have genetic evidence that they are NUA and have ancestors in the Back Cross Project). This is a genetic certainty, and you should not accept any breeder who brushes this issue off with a statement such as "My dogs have never suffered with that issue." To learn more, Google NUA or LUA Dalmatians and the Back Cross Project.

In these early growth stage recipes, we have relied more heavily on bonemeal and less on ground bone to balance calcium and phosphorus. This is due to the more critical nature of the Ca, P quantities and ratio at this age. Ground chicken wings/backs/necks and similar sources of bone suitable for grinding are, by their very nature, more variable in bone content, so using bonemeal gives more precise control. However, I appreciate that some people prefer to rely on whole foods as much as possible, so some recipes in this growth stage include ground bones. This becomes more common as you move through the book to later growth-stage recipes.

Ziggy's Duck Delight

with Mushrooms & Greens

Quick and easy. If you keep supplements in the cupboard, the rest of these ingredients will be readily available at the store. Duck eggs are not always available year-round, but if you can't get them, switch to hen eggs and add a further 18mg iron supplement (typically another capsule at 18mg/cap).

Formulated to FEDIAF. Balanced RAW or COOKED

Ingredients

3,026g Duck, no bone, 15% fat

1,041g Duck egg, whole, no shell

871g Green leafy vegetables but avoid spinach

363g Mushrooms, white or brown, but avoid shiitake

290g Yoghurt, plain, whole fat

145g Almonds

47g Brazil nuts

145g Flaxseed or Chia seed

85g Bonemeal

7g Kelp powder

7g Salt, finely ground

1,250mg Choline, typically 5 capsule at 250mg/cap

180mg Zinc, typically 12 capsules at 15mg / cap

72mg Iron, typically 4 capsules at 18mg/cap

16mg Copper, typically 8 capsules at 2mg/cap

10g Salmon oil

14g Cod liver oil

Please weigh all ingredients accurately. Cooking is optional.

You will need a large mixing bowl, tub, or small bucket and a large, sturdy, long-handled spoon to thoroughly mix the recipe.

Method

1. You will need a large mixing bowl.

2. If cooking the duck, it can be sliced and steamed or wrapped and slow-roasted at low heat in the oven. Once ready, shred straight into the mixing bowl. If raw, simply grind half straight into the bowl and chop the rest into bite-sized chunks.

3. As eggs form more than 10% of the recipe, we recommend cooking the whites to avoid any potential interference with biotin absorption. The yolks can be scrambled with the whites or put into the mixing bowl raw.

4. Chop & steam the leafy veg. Add to the bowl.

5. Chop the mushrooms and again steam or lightly saute dry or with a little water. Even if the remainder of the recipe is left raw, lightly cooking the mushrooms has nutritional benefits.

6. Add the yogurt to the bowl.

7. Chop the almonds and Brazil nuts before adding them to the mix

8. Grind the seeds and add them also

9. Now you can add all the powdered ingredients: bonemeal, kelp & salt

10. Twist open the supplement capsules and add the powder from those to the bowl

11. Roughly mix everything until no dry powders are visible

12. Add the salmon & cod liver oils, then thoroughly mix the entire recipe

13. Serve up!

Refrigerate or freeze the remainder.

See Chapt. 5 for portion sizing, Chapt. 6 for substitutions, Chapts. 8-10 for additional method details, tips, & advice, Chapt. 11 for storage info. and Chapt. 12 for online suppliers.

Nutritional Information

MACRONUTRIENT ANALYSIS			
Composition	As formulated	Dry Matter	% kcal
Protein	13%	40%	28%
Fat	13%	41%	68%
Ash	3%	8%	
Moisture	68%		
Fiber	2%	5%	
Net Carbs	2%	6%	4%
Sugars	1%	3%	2%
Starch	1%	2%	1%
Total			

MACRONUTRIENT INFORMATION	
Total kcal in recipe	10,000
kcal / oz	46
kcal / lb	742
kcal / 100g	164
kcal / kg	1,635

MINERALS				
	Unit	Min	Max	Recipe
Ca	g	2.5	4	2.99
P	g	2.25		2.35
Ca:P	ratio	1:1	1.8:1	1.27:1
K	g	1.1		1.81
Na	g	0.55		0.79
MG	g	0.1		0.25
Cl	g	0.83		0.9
Fe	mg	22	350	24.35
Cu	mg	2.75	7	3.21
Mn	mg	1.4	40	2
Zn	mg	25	70	26.93
I	mg	0.38	3	0.53
Se	mg	0.1		0.18

VITAMINS				
	Unit	Min	Max	Recipe
Vit A	IU	1,250		4506.63
Vit C	mg			18.52
Vit D	IU	138		260.59
Vit E	IU	12.5		12.5
Thiamine, B1	mg	0.45		0.86
Riboflavine, B2	mg	1.05		1.55
Niacin, B3	mg	3.4		24.1
Pantothenic Acid, B5	mg	3		6.34
B6 (Pyridoxine)	mg	0.3		0.61
Vit B12	mg	0.01		0
Folic Acid	mg	0.05		0.17
Choline	mg	425		434.07
Vit K1	mg			0.29
Biotin	mg			0.26

FATS				
	Unit	Min	Max	Recipe
Total	g	21.25		80.37
Saturated	g			20.79
Monounsaturated	g			37.73
Polyunsaturated	g			14.2
LA	g	3.25	16.25	9.26
ALA	g	0.2		3.32
AA	g	0.08		0.35
EPA	g			0.24
DPA	g			0.01
DHA	g			0.22
Omega-6/Omega-3	ratio			2.32 : 1
EPA + DHA	g	0.13		0.46

AMINO ACIDS				
	Unit	Min	Max	Recipe
Total protein	g	62.5		79.1
Tryptophan	g	0.58		1.09
Threonine	g	2.03		3.49
Isoleucine	g	1.63		3.8
Leucine	g	3.23		6.29
Lysine*	g	2.2	7*	6.03
Methionine	g	0.88		2.26
M - Cystine	g	1.75		3.48
Phenylalanine	g	1.63		3.73
P - Tyrosine	g	3.25		6.67
Valine	g	1.7		4.26
Arginine	g	2.05		5.2
Histidine	g	0.98		2
Purines	mg			589.34
Taurine	g			0.49

NB kcal per weight values will vary according to cooking or if raw. The values given are based on cooked as per the recipe.

Perdie's Tripe & Chicken

With Blueberries

Perdie is the quintessential Dalmatian girl's name, thanks to Disney. Dalmatians are intelligent, playful, energetic, and loving. They need a low-purine diet, regular training, and plenty of exercise but will reward you with intense loyalty and huge smiles. If you have never seen a Dally smile, Google it!

Formulated to FEDIAF. Balanced RAW

Ingredients

4,045g Beef Tripe

2,842g Chicken meat, no skin or bone

958g Chicken wings incl. skin & bone

1,137g Egg, no shell

576g Blueberries

54g Turmeric powder

33g Bonemeal

7g Salt finely ground

5g Kelp powder, (I = 700mcg/g)

210mg Zinc, typically 14 capsules at 15mg / cap

90mg Iron, typically 5 capsules at 18mg / cap

28mg Copper, e.g. 14 capsules at 2mg / cap

59g Cod liver oil

Please weigh all ingredients accurately. Cooking is optional.

Method

1. Place tripe into a large mixing bowl. If it didn't come minced, grind it first.

2. Chop chicken breast into bite-sized chunks and add to bowl

3. Grind chicken wings and add to the bowl

4. As eggs are more than 10% of the recipe, you may like to separate the whites and poach before adding them to avoid any concerns about biotin absorption.

5. Add blueberries. If you start helping yourself with a few, take them from the packet, not the weighed-out portion!

6. Now you can add all the powdered ingredients: turmeric, salt, kelp

7. Twist open the supplement capsules and add the powder from those to the bowl

8. Roughly mix everything until no dry powders are visible

9. Add the cod liver oil, then thoroughly mix the entire recipe

10. Weigh out a suitably sized portion to serve to your puppy.

For the best long-term health, practice body condition scoring, use the growth charts, and try not to over- or underfeed. Refrigerate or freeze the remainder.

See Chapt. 5 for growth charts and portion sizing, Chapt. 6 for substitutions, Chapts. 8-10 for additional method details, tips, & advice, Chapt. 11 for storage info. and Chapt. 12 for online suppliers.

Nutritional Information

MACRONUTRIENT ANALYSIS			
Composition	As formulated	Dry Matter	% kcal
Protein	15%	63%	52%
Fat	5%	20%	41%
Ash	2%	8%	
Moisture	75%		
Fiber	0%	1%	
Net Carbs	2%	8%	7%
Sugars	1%	3%	3%
Starch	0%	2%	1%
Total			100%

MACRONUTRIENT INFORMATION				
Total kcal in recipe				
kcal / oz				
kcal / lb				
kcal / 100g				
kcal / kg				

MINERALS				
	Unit	Min	Max	Recipe
Ca	g	2.5	4	
P	g	2.25		
Ca:P	ratio	1:1	1.8:1	
K	g	1.1		
Na	g	0.55		
MG	g	0.1		
Cl	g	0.83		
Fe	mg	22	350	
Cu	mg	2.75	7	
Mn	mg	1.4	40	
Zn	mg	25	70	
I	mg	0.38	3	
Se	mg	0.1		

VITAMINS				
	Unit	Min	Max	Recipe
Vit A	IU	1,250		
Vit C	mg			
Vit D	IU	138		
Vit E	IU	12.5		
Thiamine, B1	mg	0.45		
Riboflavine, B2	mg	1.05		
Niacin, B3	mg	3.4		
Pantothenic Acid, B5	mg	3		
B6 (Pyridoxine)	mg	0.3		
Vit B12	mg	0.01		
Folic Acid	mg	0.05		
Choline	mg	425		
Vit K1	mg			
Biotin	mg			

FATS				
	Unit	Min	Max	Recipe
Total	g	21.25		
Saturated	g			
Monounsaturated	g			
Polyunsaturated	g			
LA	g	3.25	16.25	
ALA	g	0.2		
AA	g	0.08		
EPA	g			
DPA	g			
DHA	g			
Omega-6/Omega-3	ratio			
EPA + DHA	g	0.13		

AMINO ACIDS				
	Unit	Min	Max	Recipe
Total protein	g	62.5		
Tryptophan	g	0.58		
Threonine	g	2.03		
Isoleucine	g	1.63		
Leucine	g	3.23		
Lysine*	g	2.2	7*	
Methionine	g	0.88		
M - Cystine	g	1.75		
Phenylalanine	g	1.63		
P - Tyrosine	g	3.25		
Valine	g	1.7		
Arginine	g	2.05		
Histidine	g	0.98		
Purines	mg			
Taurine	g			

RAW. Puppies from 50% to 80% adult weight.

Likely from around 14-16 weeks old.

These recipes have been balanced based on ingredients being left raw.

The puppy weight for these recipes is between 50% and 80% of their final anticipated adult weight. This likely means your puppy is over 14 weeks old, but the upper age depends upon the breed. See Chapter 5 for more information about different growth phases, growth charts, and how to score body condition.

You can always 'step back' and feed recipes for the previous growth stage section; just don't jump forward to an older age group recipe. This means that as your puppy grows, you have more recipe options available to you.

Monty's Beefy Beans
& Egg

Chickpeas are beneficial for a puppy's microbiome, but they should not be introduced in the first 14 weeks; hence, this is their first appearance so far. For particularly small pups, you could mash them before adding them.

Formulated to FEDIAF

Ingredients

3,780g Beef, ground, 10% fat

300g Beef liver

227g Beef kidney

523g Chicken wings incl. bones

181g Oysters

340g Eggs, no shell

567g Chickpeas, garbanzo beans, cooked weight

252g Brussell sprouts

57g Bonemeal

45g Parsley, dried

166g Spirulina powder

6g Kelp powder (I = 700mcg/g)

5g Salt

21g Cod liver oil

Please weigh all ingredients accurately.

This recipe requires a meat grinder that can cope with poultry bones.

You will need a large mixing bowl, tub, or small bucket and a large, sturdy, long-handled spoon to thoroughly mix the recipe.

Method

1. Start by placing the ground beef base in a large mixing bowl or bucket

2. Grind the chicken wings and add to the bowl

3. Chop liver, kidney & oysters into bite-sized chunks, then add to bowl

4. Crack the fresh eggs straight into the mix

5. Add the cooked chickpeas

6. Finely chop the Brussels or run them through a juicer and add juice and pulp to the bowl.

7. Next, add all the powdered ingredients: bonemeal, parsley, spirulina, kelp & salt.

8. Roughly mix everything until no dry powders are visible

9. Add the cod liver oil, then thoroughly mix the entire recipe

10. Weigh out a suitably sized portion to serve to your puppy.

For the best long-term health, practice body condition scoring, use the growth charts, and try not to over- or underfeed. Refrigerate or freeze the remainder.

See Chapt. 5 for growth charts and portion sizing, Chapt. 6 for substitutions, Chapts. 8-10 for additional method details, tips, & advice, Chapt. 11 for storage info. and Chapt. 12 for online suppliers.

Nutritional Information

MACRONUTRIENT ANALYSIS			
Composition	As formulated	Dry Matter	% kcal
Protein	18.17%	57.45%	47.01%
Fat	8.33%	26.34%	48.49%
Ash	2.48%	7.84%	
Moisture	68.37%		
Fiber	0.91%	2.88%	
Net Carbs	1.74%	5.49%	4.49%
Sugars	0.45%	1.44%	1.18%
Starch	0.23%	0.73%	0.59%
Total			100%

MACRONUTRIENT INFORMATION					
Total kcal in recipe					10,000
kcal / oz					44
kcal / lb					701
kcal / 100g					155
kcal / kg					1,546

MINERALS				
	Unit	Min	Max	Recipe
Ca	g	2.5	5	2.65
P	g	2.25		2.27
Ca:P	ratio	1:1	1.8:1	1.17 : 1
K	g	1.1		2.07
Na	g	0.55		0.96
MG	g	0.1		0.2
Cl	g	0.83		0.96
Fe	mg	22	350	23.23
Cu	mg	2.75	7	4.47
Mn	mg	1.4	40	1.59
Zn	mg	25	70	28.13
I	mg	0.38	3	0.4
Se	mg	0.1		0.13

VITAMINS				
	Unit	Min	Max	Recipe
Vit A	IU	1,250		6,042.17
Vit C	mg			28.29
Vit D	IU	138		414.57
Vit E	IU	12.5		13.2
Thiamine, B1	mg	0.45		0.82
Riboflavine, B2	mg	1.05		2.9
Niacin, B3	mg	3.4		29.27
Pantothenic Acid, B5	mg	3		6.96
B6 (Pyridoxine)	mg	0.3		2.5
Vit B12	mg	0.01		0.04
Folic Acid	mg	0.05		0.22
Choline	mg	425		543.92
Vit K1	mg			0.11
Biotin	mg			0.43

FATS				
	Unit	Min	Max	Recipe
Total	g	21.25		53.88
Saturated	g			19.37
Monounsaturated	g			21.09
Polyunsaturated	g			5.04
LA	g	3.25	16.25	3.27
ALA	g	0.2		0.46
AA	g	0.08		0.4
EPA	g			0.26
DPA	g			0.06
DHA	g			0.31
Omega-6/Omega-3	ratio			3.43 : 1
EPA + DHA	g	0.13		0.58

AMINO ACIDS				
	Unit	Min	Max	Recipe
Total protein	g	62.5		117.53
Tryptophan	g	0.58		0.91
Threonine	g	2.03		4.66
Isoleucine	g	1.63		5.37
Leucine	g	3.23		9.28
Lysine*	g	2.2	7*	9.25
Methionine	g	0.88		2.93
M - Cystine	g	1.75		4.25
Phenylalanine	g	1.63		4.86
P - Tyrosine	g	3.25		8.7
Valine	g	1.7		6
Arginine	g	2.05		7.72
Histidine	g	0.98		3.6
Purines	mg			717.97
Taurine	g			0.17

Conker's Catfish

& Edamame

Good for the guts! Fish is often more readily digested by puppies with delicate tummies, and Catfish is one of the more affordable options. Edamame beans support a healthy microbiome, aiding settled digestion in puppies that are more susceptible to tummy upsets.

Formulated to FEDIAF

5,543g Catfish

635g Chicken necks

707g Lamb heart

248g Beef liver

625g Oysters

715g Egg, whole, no shell

794g Edamame, frozen or canned, pre-cooked

476g Green leafy veg.

42g Hemp seeds

277g Spirulina powder

86g Turmeric powder

80g Bonemeal

12g Salt

7g Kelp powder

31g Olive oil

Please weigh all ingredients accurately.

This recipe requires a meat grinder that can cope with poultry bones.

You will need a large mixing bowl, tub, or small bucket and a large, sturdy, long-handled spoon to thoroughly mix the recipe.

Method

1. Grind half of the catfish, along with the chicken necks, heart, liver, and oysters, in a large mixing bowl.

2. Chop the remainder of the catfish into bite-sized chunks and add to the bowl.

3. Crack the eggs straight into the bowl and add the edamame beans

4. Chop or juice the leafy greens and add both pulp and juice into the mix

5. Grind the hempseeds before adding them to the bowl

6. Now add all the powdered ingredients: spirulina, turmeric, bonemeal, salt & kelp.

7. Roughly mix everything until no dry powders are visible

8. Add the olive oil, then thoroughly mix the entire recipe

9. Serve up!

For the best long-term health, practice body condition scoring, use the growth charts, and try not to over- or underfeed. Refrigerate or freeze the remainder.

See Chapt. 5 for growth charts and portion sizing, Chapt. 6 for substitutions, Chapts. 8-10 for additional method details, tips, & advice, Chapt. 11 for storage info. and Chapt. 12 for online suppliers.

Nutritional Information

MACRONUTRIENT ANALYSIS			
Composition	As formulated	Dry Matter	% kcal
Protein	15.9%	63.97%	57.2%
Fat	4.27%	17.2%	37.34%
Ash	2.33%	9.36%	
Moisture	75.14%		
Fiber	0.83%	3.36%	
Net Carbs	1.52%	6.12%	5.47%
Sugars	0.51%	2.06%	1.85%
Starch	0.84%	3.38%	3.02%
Total			100%

MACRONUTRIENT INFORMATION	
Total kcal in recipe	10,000
kcal / oz	28
kcal / lb	441
kcal / 100g	97
kcal / kg	973

MINERALS				
	Unit	Min	Max	Recipe
Ca	g	2.5	5	3.59
P	g	2.25		3.45
Ca:P	ratio	1:1	1.8:1	1.04 : 1
K	g	1.1		3.8
Na	g	0.55		1.42
MG	g	0.1		0.43
Cl	g	0.83		1.23
Fe	mg	22	350	28.65
Cu	mg	2.75	7	6.88
Mn	mg	1.4	40	4.21
Zn	mg	25	70	33.16
I	mg	0.38	3	0.59
Se	mg	0.1		0.16

VITAMINS				
	Unit	Min	Max	Recipe
Vit A	IU	1,250		7,653.97
Vit C	mg			32.35
Vit D	IU	138		2,891.15
Vit E	IU	12.5		14.78
Thiamine, B1	mg	0.45		2.51
Riboflavine, B2	mg	1.05		3.59
Niacin, B3	mg	3.4		27.71
Pantothenic Acid, B5	mg	3		11.33
B6 (Pyridoxine)	mg	0.3		1.75
Vit B12	mg	0.01		0.05
Folic Acid	mg	0.05		0.54
Choline	mg	425		471.53
Vit K1	mg			0.22
Biotin	mg			0.47

FATS				
	Unit	Min	Max	Recipe
Total	g	21.25		43.92
Saturated	g			11.41
Monounsaturated	g			13.81
Polyunsaturated	g			12.09
LA	g	3.25	16.25	5.33
ALA	g	0.2		1.36
AA	g	0.08		1.11
EPA	g			1
DPA	g			0.61
DHA	g			1.54
Omega-6/Omega-3	ratio			1.63 : 1
EPA + DHA	g	0.13		2.54

AMINO ACIDS				
	Unit	Min	Max	Recipe
Total protein	g	62.5		163.42
Tryptophan	g	0.58		1.93
Threonine	g	2.03		6.99
Isoleucine	g	1.63		7.55
Leucine	g	3.23		13.09
Lysine*	g	2.2	7*	13.23
Methionine	g	0.88		4.3
M - Cystine	g	1.75		6.22
Phenylalanine	g	1.63		6.79
P - Tyrosine	g	3.25		12.47
Valine	g	1.7		8.44
Arginine	g	2.05		10.24
Histidine	g	0.98		4.37
Purines	mg			506.05
Taurine	g			0.14

Roza's Chicken & Chicory

With Salmon

Chicory is rich in vitamin K and folate and, along with sweet potato, is known for settling upset tummies. Chicken gizzards add an excellent range of minerals and vitamins. If you can't find them, you can leave them out and add an additional 12g of oysters to re-balance, but be aware that the calories will be reduced.

Formulated to FEDIAF

4,329g Chicken meat, no skin or bone

1082g Chicken legs or thighs with meat, skin and bone

534g Chicken gizzards

396g Oysters

271g Beef liver

866g Salmon with bones, canned, fresh, or frozen

810g Sweet potato

374g Chicory, escarole, endive

113g Sunflower or safflower seeds

117g Spirulina powder

104g Turmeric powder

54g Bonemeal

6g Kelp powder

4g Salt

3g Cod liver oil

Please weigh all ingredients accurately.

This recipe requires a meat grinder that can cope with poultry bones.

You will need a large mixing bowl, tub, or small bucket and a large, sturdy, long-handled spoon to thoroughly mix the recipe.

Method

1. Chop approx. half the chicken meat into bite-sized chunks and place in a large mixing bowl.

2. Grind the remainder of the chicken meat, along with the whole legs, gizzards, oysters, and liver, in a bowl.

3. If the salmon is canned, simply add it to the bowl. If it is fresh, chop it into bite-sized chunks before adding it.

4. To make the sweet potato's nutrients more bioavailable, you can either lightly steam and then mash it or put it raw through a juicer, adding both pulp and juice to the mixing bowl.

5. If you have the juicer running, pop the chicory through as well. If not, finely chop it and add it raw to the mix.

6. Grind the sunflower seeds and add to mix.

7. Next, add the powdered ingredients: spirulina, turmeric, bonemeal, kelp & salt.

8. Roughly mix everything until no dry powders are visible

9. Add the cod liver oil, then thoroughly mix the entire recipe

10. Ready for Roza! Or whoever your pupsie happens to be :)

Practice body condition scoring, use the growth charts, and try not to over or under-feed for the best long-term health. Refrigerate or freeze the remainder.

See Chapt. 5 for growth charts and portion sizing, Chapt. 6 for substitutions, Chapts. 8-10 for additional method details, tips, & advice, Chapt. 11 for storage info. and Chapt. 12 for online suppliers.

Nutritional Information

MACRONUTRIENT ANALYSIS			
Composition	As formulated	Dry Matter	% kcal
Protein	18.68%	65.3%	59.24%
Fat	4.26%	14.89%	32.81%
Ash	2.29%	8.02%	
Moisture	71.39%		
Fiber	0.86%	3.02%	
Net Carbs	2.51%	8.77%	7.95%
Sugars	0.61%	2.14%	1.94%
Starch	2.06%	7.22%	6.55%
Total			100%

MACRONUTRIENT INFORMATION				
Total kcal in recipe				10,000
kcal / oz				31
kcal / lb				501
kcal / 100g				110
kcal / kg				1,104

MINERALS				
	Unit	Min	Max	Recipe
Ca	g	2.5	5	3.22
P	g	2.25		3.15
Ca:P	ratio	1:1	1.8:1	1.02 : 1
K	g	1.1		2.86
Na	g	0.55		0.84
MG	g	0.1		0.39
Cl	g	0.83		0.98
Fe	mg	22	350	23.66
Cu	mg	2.75	7	4.9
Mn	mg	1.4	40	3.63
Zn	mg	25	70	25
I	mg	0.38	3	0.46
Se	mg	0.1		0.17

VITAMINS				
	Unit	Min	Max	Recipe
Vit A	IU	1,250		14,390.11
Vit C	mg			15.1
Vit D	IU	138		623.81
Vit E	IU	12.5		15.59
Thiamine, B1	mg	0.45		0.97
Riboflavine, B2	mg	1.05		2.35
Niacin, B3	mg	3.4		65.14
Pantothenic Acid, B5	mg	3		9.94
B6 (Pyridoxine)	mg	0.3		3.81
Vit B12	mg	0.01		0.03
Folic Acid	mg	0.05		0.21
Choline	mg	425		636.56
Vit K1	mg			0.1
Biotin	mg			0.48

FATS				
	Unit	Min	Max	Recipe
Total	g	21.25		38.6
Saturated	g			10
Monounsaturated	g			12.74
Polyunsaturated	g			10.34
LA	g	3.25	16.25	6.59
ALA	g	0.2		0.34
AA	g	0.08		0.65
EPA	g			0.61
DPA	g			0.17
DHA	g			0.91
Omega-6/Omega-3	ratio			3.95 : 1
EPA + DHA	g	0.13		1.52

AMINO ACIDS				
	Unit	Min	Max	Recipe
Total protein	g	62.5		169.26
Tryptophan	g	0.58		2.02
Threonine	g	2.03		7.34
Isoleucine	g	1.63		8.54
Leucine	g	3.23		12.97
Lysine*	g	2.2	7*	14.01
Methionine	g	0.88		4.52
M - Cystine	g	1.75		6.62
Phenylalanine	g	1.63		6.97
P - Tyrosine	g	3.25		12.81
Valine	g	1.7		8.67
Arginine	g	2.05		10.91
Histidine	g	0.98		5.04
Purines	mg			1,346.78
Taurine	g			0.33

Spooky's Beef

& Salmon

You may have noticed more recipes with real bone in this section. Now that the pups have moved into a different mineral requirement growth range, we can start getting them used to bone without the risk of the natural variation exceeding calcium limits. We still utilize ground bonemeal to balance the final level and ratio to phosphorous.

Formulated to AAFCO.

Ingredients

2,772g Chicken meat, 85% lean

647g Chicken wings

462g Beef heart

240g Beef liver

785g Salmon, canned, fresh, or frozen with bones

277g Egg, whole, no shell

785g Broccoli

186g Sunflower or Safflower seeds

59g Bonemeal

38g Nutritional yeast

42g Cloves, ground

10g Salt

7g Kelp

165mg Zinc, e.g. 11 capsules at 15mg/cap

126mg Iron, e.g. 7 capsules at 18mg/cap

Please weigh all ingredients accurately.

This recipe requires a meat grinder that can cope with poultry bones.

You will need a large mixing bowl, tub, or small bucket and a large, sturdy, long-handled spoon to thoroughly mix the recipe.

Method

1. Chop approx. Half to two-thirds of the salmon and chicken meat into bite-sized chunks and place in the mixing bowl

2. Grind the remainder along with the chicken wings, beef heart and liver, Add to the bowl.

3. Add the eggs to the mix.

4. Juice the broccoli and add both juice and pulp to the mix. If you have no juicer, chop the florets and grate the stem.

5. Grind the seeds

6. Now add all the dry powdered ingredients: bonemeal, yeast, cloves, salt & kelp.

7. Twist open any supplement capsules and sprinkle the powder into the bowl

8. Roughly mix everything until no dry powders are visible

9. Add the cod liver oil, then thoroughly mix the entire recipe

10. Weigh out a suitably sized portion to serve to your puppy.

For the best long-term health, practice body condition scoring, use the growth charts, and try not to over- or underfeed. Refrigerate or freeze the remainder.

See Chapt. 5 for growth charts and portion sizing, Chapt. 6 for substitutions, Chapts. 8-10 for additional method details, tips, & advice, Chapt. 11 for storage info. and Chapt. 12 for online suppliers.

Nutritional Information

MACRONUTRIENT ANALYSIS				
Composition		As formulated	Dry Matter	% kcal
Protein		17.05%	51.45%	37.75%
Fat		10.9%	32.9%	58.64%
Ash		2.59%	7.8%	
Moisture		66.87%		
Fiber		0.97%	2.93%	
Net Carbs		1.63%	4.92%	3.61%
Sugars		0.57%	1.72%	1.26%
Starch		0.81%	2.44%	1.79%
Total				100%

MACRONUTRIENT INFORMATION				
Total kcal in recipe				10,000
kcal / oz				45
kcal / lb				717
kcal / 100g				158
kcal / kg				1,580

MINERALS				
	Unit	Min	Max	Recipe
Ca	g	3	4.5	3
P	g	2.5	4	2.64
Ca:P	ratio	1:1	2:1	1.13 : 1
K	g	1.5		1.72
Na	g	0.8		0.89
MG	g	0.15		0.28
Cl	g	1.1		1.16
Fe	mg	22		22.1
Cu	mg	3.1		3.11
Mn	mg	1.8		2.46
Zn	mg	25		26.47
I	mg	0.25	2.75	0.49
Se	mg	0.09		0.12

VITAMINS				
	Unit	Min	Max	Recipe
Vit A	IU	1,250	62,500	4,897.78
Vit C	mg			80.16
Vit D	IU	125	750	563.93
Vit E	IU	12.5		17.95
Thiamine, B1	mg	0.56		3.22
Riboflavine, B2	mg	1.3		4.45
Niacin, B3	mg	3.4		43.88
Pantothenic Acid, B5	mg	3		7.83
B6 (Pyridoxine)	mg	0.38		4.07
Vit B12	mg	0.01		0.03
Folic Acid	mg	0.05		0.41
Choline	mg	340		476.56
Vit K1	mg			0.09
Biotin	mg			0.45

FATS				
	Unit	Min	Max	Recipe
Total	g	21.3		68.99
Saturated	g			18.16
Monounsaturated	g			24.55
Polyunsaturated	g			17.29
LA	g	3.3		12.97
ALA	g	0.2		0.56
AA	g	0.08		1
EPA	g			0.45
DPA	g			0.22
DHA	g			0.84
Omega-6/Omega-3	ratio		30:1	7.56:1
EPA + DHA	g	0.1		1.28

AMINO ACIDS				
	Unit	Min	Max	Recipe
Total protein	g	56.3		107.87
Tryptophan	g	0.5		1.25
Threonine	g	2.6		4.7
Isoleucine	g	1.78		5.06
Leucine	g	3.23		8.41
Lysine*	g	2.25		9.06
Methionine	g	0.88		2.93
M - Cystine	g	1.75		4.18
Phenylalanine	g	2.08		4.41
P - Tyrosine	g	3.25		8.16
Valine	g	1.7		5.51
Arginine	g	2.5		7.24
Histidine	g	1.1		3.24
Purines	mg			796.5
Taurine	g			0.66

Rufus' Duck
& Mushrooms

Rufus went to live with another vet who did her thesis at Vet School on the Back-cross project. This breeding project corrects Dalmatians' genetic defects by tracking a missing gene through breeding stock. She knew she was looking for Rufus before his birth because he carries a precious copy of the vital corrective gene.

Formulated to FEDIAF

Ingredients

3,059g Duck, whole with bone & skin

603g Duck or chicken liver

603g Duck egg, whole, no shell

406g Oysters

394g Mushrooms, Button or Portobello

69g Carrots

75g Brazil nuts

75g Nutritional yeast

88g Turmeric Powder

31g Spirulina powder

8g Bonemeal

5g Kelp powder (I = 700mcg/g)

4g Salt

16g Cod liver oil

Please weigh all ingredients accurately.

This recipe requires a meat grinder that can cope with poultry bones.

You will need a large mixing bowl, tub, or small bucket and a large, sturdy, long-handled spoon to thoroughly mix the recipe.

Method

1. Cut off the main muscle meat from the ducks—just the easy stuff, the breasts, and main leg meat. Chop this into bite-sized chunks and place it in your mixing bowl.

2. The rest of the duck, including skin, bone, and liver, should be put through the grinder. Then, add it to the bowl.

3. Add the eggs and oysters to the mix.

4. Grate the carrots before adding them to the mix. It is not worth dirtying the juicer for this amount of carrots, but they balance some of the required vitamins.

5. Even if you keep the rest raw, chop and lightly cook the mushrooms. Add to the mix.

6. Chop the Brazils and add to the bowl.

7. Now add all the dry powdered ingredients: yeast, turmeric, spirulina, bonemeal, salt & kelp.

8. Roughly mix everything until no dry powders are visible

9. Add the cod liver oil, then thoroughly mix the entire recipe

10. Weigh out a suitably sized portion to serve to your puppy.

For the best long-term health, practice body condition scoring, use the growth charts, and try not to over- or underfeed. Refrigerate or freeze the remainder.

See Chapt. 5 for growth charts and portion sizing, Chapt. 6 for substitutions, Chapts. 8-10 for additional method details, tips, & advice, Chapt. 11 for storage info. and Chapt. 12 for online suppliers.

Nutritional Information

MACRONUTRIENT ANALYSIS			
Composition	As formulated	Dry Matter	% kcal
Protein	16%	45.63%	34.76%
Fat	12.23%	34.86%	59.76%
Ash	3.1%	8.85%	
Moisture	64.93%		
Fiber	1.22%	3.47%	
Net Carbs	2.52%	7.2%	5.48%
Sugars	0.99%	2.83%	2.16%
Starch	1.35%	3.84%	2.92%
Total			100%

MACRONUTRIENT INFORMATION					
Total kcal in recipe					10,000
kcal / oz					52
kcal / lb					835
kcal / 100g					184
kcal / kg					1,841

MINERALS				
	Unit	Min	Max	Recipe
Ca	g	2.5	5	3.42
P	g	2.25		3.22
Ca:P	ratio	1:1	1.8:1	1.06 : 1
K	g	1.1		1.11
Na	g	0.55		0.77
MG	g	0.1		0.22
Cl	g	0.83		0.9
Fe	mg	22	350	27.07
Cu	mg	2.75	7	2.95
Mn	mg	1.4	40	2.49
Zn	mg	25	70	25.02
I	mg	0.38	3	0.39
Se	mg	0.1		0.27

VITAMINS				
	Unit	Min	Max	Recipe
Vit A	IU	1,250		20,365.42
Vit C	mg			15.7
Vit D	IU	138		338.47
Vit E	IU	12.5		13.35
Thiamine, B1	mg	0.45		6.64
Riboflavine, B2	mg	1.05		7.6
Niacin, B3	mg	3.4		60.31
Pantothenic Acid, B5	mg	3		10.73
B6 (Pyridoxine)	mg	0.3		5.51
Vit B12	mg	0.01		0.04
Folic Acid	mg	0.05		0.87
Choline	mg	425		470.91
Vit K1	mg			0.01
Biotin	mg			0.91

FATS				
	Unit	Min	Max	Recipe
Total	g	21.25		66.4
Saturated	g			19.66
Monounsaturated	g			31.23
Polyunsaturated	g			9.35
LA	g	3.25	16.25	7.33
ALA	g	0.2		0.43
AA	g	0.08		0.4
EPA	g			0.28
DPA	g			0.04
DHA	g			0.32
Omega-6/Omega-3	ratio			7.42 : 1
EPA + DHA	g	0.13		0.59

AMINO ACIDS				
	Unit	Min	Max	Recipe
Total protein	g	62.5		86.9
Tryptophan	g	0.58		1.14
Threonine	g	2.03		3.79
Isoleucine	g	1.63		4.22
Leucine	g	3.23		6.99
Lysine*	g	2.2	7*	6.88
Methionine	g	0.88		2.41
M - Cystine	g	1.75		3.69
Phenylalanine	g	1.63		3.95
P - Tyrosine	g	3.25		7.16
Valine	g	1.7		4.72
Arginine	g	2.05		5.52
Histidine	g	0.98		2.27
Purines	mg			656.66
Taurine	g			0.56

COOKED or RAW. Puppies from 50% to 80% adult weight

Likely from around 14 to 16 weeks old.

Cooking is optional. These recipes have all been formulated and nutritionally balanced based on whether ingredients remain raw or are cooked. See Chapter 8 for more details about cooking methods.

The puppy weight for these recipes is between 50% and 80% of their final anticipated adult weight. This likely means your puppy is over 14 weeks old, but the upper age depends upon the breed. See Chapter 5 for more information about different growth phases, growth charts, and how to score body condition.

Although values for kcals per recipe weight are provided, these will vary according to the final finished recipe weight, which varies according to water content after cooking. To calculate more accurate values if you cook a recipe, please see Chapter 12.

You can always 'step back' and feed recipes for the previous growth stage section; don't jump forward to an older age group recipe.

In all recipes that might be cooked, we do not include natural sources of bone such as poultry wings, necks, and backs because cooked poultry bone can lead to sharp shards with potential internal injury or obstruction risks.

Sam's Seafood

& Chickpeas

If you live in the right place, seafood can be affordable and readily available. It is highly nutritious, but not all dogs love it. We have a collie who really isn't keen on fish or seafood-rich recipes. Our Dallies are very happy about that and willing to help by clearing any leftovers for her!

Formulated to FEDIAF

Ingredients

2,943g Shrimp

1,471g Fish roe, mixed species

1,471g Salmon

736g Oysters

258g Green leafy vegetables

589g Chickpeas, garbanzo beans, canned or cooked

124g Chia or Flax seeds

91g Bonemeal

41g Parsley, dried

41g Turmeric powder

41g Spirulina powder

27g Hempseed oil

9g Salt

7g Kelp powder

72mg Iron, e.g. 4 capsules at 18mg/cap

Please weigh all ingredients accurately.

Method – cooking is optional

1. Steam all the fish and seafood until just cooked & opaque.

2. Leave the shrimps whole or half according to your puppy's size. Add to the bowl.

3. Shred salmon and add to bowl along with the roe and oysters

4. Chop and steam the leafy greens and add to the bowl

5. Mash the beans to aid binding and add them to the mixture

6. Grind the seeds before adding them

7. Now add all the dry powdered ingredients: bonemeal, parsley, turmeric, spirulina, salt & kelp.

8. Twist open iron supplement capsules and sprinkle the powder into the bowl

9. Roughly mix everything until no dry powders are visible

10. Add the hempseed oil, then thoroughly mix the entire recipe

11. If it is too dry, you can add water, but just be aware this will affect the overall recipe weight.

12. Ready for serving.

For the best long-term health, practice body condition scoring, use the growth charts, and try not to over- or underfeed. Refrigerate or freeze the remainder.

See Chapt. 5 for growth charts and portion sizing, Chapt. 6 for substitutions, Chapts. 8-10 for additional method details, tips, & advice, Chapt. 11 for storage info. and Chapt. 12 for online suppliers.

Nutritional Information

MACRONUTRIENT ANALYSIS			
Composition	As formulated	Dry Matter	% kcal
Protein	20.15%	66.74%	63.33%
Fat	4.33%	14.36%	30.65%
Ash	2.62%	8.67%	
Moisture	69.81%		
Fiber	1.17%	3.88%	
Net Carbs	1.92%	6.35%	6.02%
Sugars	0.14%	0.47%	0.45%
Starch	1%	3.3%	3.13%
Total			100%

MACRONUTRIENT INFORMATION					
Total kcal in recipe					10,000
kcal / oz					36
kcal / lb					577
kcal / 100g					127
kcal / kg					1,272

MINERALS				
	Unit	Min	Max	Recipe
Ca	g	2.5	5	3.33
P	g	2.25		3.33
Ca:P	ratio	1:1	1.8:1	1.00 : 1
K	g	1.1		2.46
Na	g	0.55		1.4
MG	g	0.1		0.36
Cl	g	0.83		1.36
Fe	mg	22	350	22.03
Cu	mg	2.75	7	3.83
Mn	mg	1.4	40	2.85
Zn	mg	25	70	35.52
I	mg	0.38	3	0.63
Se	mg	0.1		0.32

VITAMINS				
	Unit	Min	Max	Recipe
Vit A	IU	1,250		2,058.41
Vit C	mg			33.82
Vit D	IU	138		994.44
Vit E	IU	12.5		16.13
Thiamine, B1	mg	0.45		0.6
Riboflavine, B2	mg	1.05		1.77
Niacin, B3	mg	3.4		28.98
Pantothenic Acid, B5	mg	3		4.23
B6 (Pyridoxine)	mg	0.3		0.87
Vit B12	mg	0.01		0.03
Folic Acid	mg	0.05		0.19
Choline	mg	425		624.62
Vit K1	mg			0.13
Biotin	mg			0.18

FATS				
	Unit	Min	Max	Recipe
Total	g	21.25		34.05
Saturated	g			6.51
Monounsaturated	g			8.86
Polyunsaturated	g			13.82
LA	g	3.25	16.25	3.27
ALA	g	0.2		3.13
AA	g	0.08		0.41
EPA	g			2.38
DPA	g			0.3
DHA	g			3.27
Omega-6/Omega-3	ratio			0.41:1
EPA + DHA	g	0.13		5.65

AMINO ACIDS				
	Unit	Min	Max	Recipe
Total protein	g	62.5		158.32
Tryptophan	g	0.58		1.81
Threonine	g	2.03		6.75
Isoleucine	g	1.63		7.49
Leucine	g	3.23		13.09
Lysine*	g	2.2	7*	13.12
Methionine	g	0.88		4.25
M - Cystine	g	1.75		6.28
Phenylalanine	g	1.63		6.9
P - Tyrosine	g	3.25		13.15
Valine	g	1.7		8.05
Arginine	g	2.05		11.63
Histidine	g	0.98		3.84
Purines	mg			532.66
Taurine	g			0.16

NB kcal per weight values will vary according to cooking or if raw. The values given are based on cooked as per the recipe.

Bernie's Beef

& Pumpkin

Bernie was our family dog when I was growing up. He was a Bernese Mountain dog and truly a gentle giant, loved by everyone. We first saw Bernese mountain dogs when skiing in Oberland in Switzerland, and the whole family fell in love with them. It was not long before we got our beautiful fluffy puppy, and he lived a full and long life until the age of 12.

Formulated to FEDIAF

Ingredients

3,125g Beef, ground, 85% lean

610g Turkey gizzards

246g Beef liver

223g Beef spleen

234g Oysters

1,116g Oily fish

313g Pumpkin

280g Spinach

134g Flax or Chia seeds

78g Bonemeal

50g Thyme, dried

46g Spirulina

8g Salt

6g Kelp powder (I = 700mcg/g)

2,800mg Choline. e.g. 8 capsules at 350mg/cap

28g Cod liver oil

7g Sunflower oil

Please weigh all ingredients accurately.

This recipe requires a meat grinder able to cope with gizzards.

You will need a large mixing bowl, tub, or small bucket and a large, sturdy, long-handled spoon to thoroughly mix the recipe.

Method – cooking is optional

1. Place the ground beef into the mixing bowl.

2. Grind the turkey gizzards, beef liver, spleen & oysters and add them to the bowl.

3. Chop the oily fish into bite-sized chunks according to puppy size and add to the bowl.

4. Divide the mixture into one or multiple roasting tins, crockery pots, or casserole dishes, and slow cook in the oven at 212F/100C for 3 to 4 hours.

5. Once the meat & fish mix is cooked, allow it to cool, and then use your hands to crumble the mix back into the bowl.

6. Chop & steam the pumpkin until just tender and add to bowl

7. Chop & briefly steam spinach to wilting point before adding it to the bowl

8. Grind the seeds and add to the mix

9. Now add all the dry powdered ingredients: bonemeal, thyme, spirulina, salt & kelp.

10. Twist open iron supplement capsules and sprinkle the powder into the bowl

11. Roughly mix everything until no dry powders are visible

12. Add the sunflower and cod liver oil, then thoroughly mix the entire recipe

13. Ready for serving.

For the best long-term health, practice body condition scoring, use the growth charts, and try not to over- or underfeed. Refrigerate or freeze the remainder.

See Chapt. 5 for growth charts and portion sizing, Chapt. 6 for substitutions, Chapts. 8-10 for additional method details, tips, & advice, Chapt. 11 for storage info. and Chapt. 12 for online suppliers.

Nutritional Information

MACRONUTRIENT ANALYSIS			
Composition	As formulated	Dry Matter	% kcal
Protein	17.27%	53.2%	39.36%
Fat	10.52%	32.4%	58.22%
Ash	2.59%	7.96%	
Moisture	67.53%		
Fiber	1.03%	3.17%	
Net Carbs	1.06%	3.27%	2.42%
Sugars	0.37%	1.14%	0.84%
Starch	0.39%	1.21%	0.9%
Total			100%

MACRONUTRIENT INFORMATION			
Total kcal in recipe			10,000
kcal / oz			44
kcal / lb			697
kcal / 100g			154
kcal / kg			1,535

MINERALS				
	Unit	Min	Max	Recipe
Ca	g	2.5	5	2.73
P	g	2.25		2.31
Ca:P	ratio	1:1	1.8:1	1.18 : 1
K	g	1.1		2.08
Na	g	0.55		0.82
MG	g	0.1		0.23
Cl	g	0.83		1.12
Fe	mg	22	350	31.75
Cu	mg	2.75	7	3.91
Mn	mg	1.4	40	1.43
Zn	mg	25	70	26.16
I	mg	0.38	3	0.46
Se	mg	0.1		0.15

VITAMINS				
	Unit	Min	Max	Recipe
Vit A	IU	1,250		8,274.36
Vit C	mg			22.92
Vit D	IU	138		571.35
Vit E	IU	12.5		12.52
Thiamine, B1	mg	0.45		0.47
Riboflavine, B2	mg	1.05		1.89
Niacin, B3	mg	3.4		31.9
Pantothenic Acid, B5	mg	3		5.26
B6 (Pyridoxine)	mg	0.3		1.17
Vit B12	mg	0.01		0.02
Folic Acid	mg	0.05		0.14
Choline	mg	425		492.26
Vit K1	mg			0.17
Biotin	mg			0.33

FATS				
	Unit	Min	Max	Recipe
Total	g	21.25		68.49
Saturated	g			25.68
Monounsaturated	g			25.93
Polyunsaturated	g			9.61
LA	g	3.25	16.25	3.26
ALA	g	0.2		3.02
AA	g	0.08		0.27
EPA	g			0.81
DPA	g			0.15
DHA	g			1.19
Omega-6/Omega-3	ratio			0.67 : 1
EPA + DHA	g	0.13		2

AMINO ACIDS				
	Unit	Min	Max	Recipe
Total protein	g	62.5		112.46
Tryptophan	g	0.58		1.19
Threonine	g	2.03		4.64
Isoleucine	g	1.63		7.76
Leucine	g	3.23		8.84
Lysine*	g	2.2	7*	9.21
Methionine	g	0.88		2.97
M - Cystine	g	1.75		4.28
Phenylalanine	g	1.63		4.57
P - Tyrosine	g	3.25		8.3
Valine	g	1.7		5.34
Arginine	g	2.05		7.11
Histidine	g	0.98		3.28
Purines	mg			735.9
Taurine	g			0.3

NB kcal per weight values will vary according to cooking or if raw. The values given are based on cooked as per the recipe.

Theo's Tripe Mix

& Poppy seeds

Theo is our son's Dalmatian, a truly gorgeous, loving boy. He comes to stay periodically and has to "rough it" in the farmhouse kitchen with his mother, sister, and auntie. Occasionally, our girls go the other way to stay at the spa (Theo's house) while we go away. They come home spoilt rotten and expecting to share our bed!

Formulated to FEDIAF

Ingredients

3,086g Beef Tripe

2,755g Chicken meat, no skin or bone

1,102g Sardines

329g Oysters

204g Beef liver

291g Sunflower seeds

110g Poppy seeds

55g Flaxseed or chia seeds

146g Turmeric powder

78g Bonemeal

22g Nutritional yeast

10g Salt

4g Kelp powder (I = 700mcg/g)

Please weigh all ingredients accurately.

You will need a large mixing bowl, tub, or small bucket and a large, sturdy, long-handled spoon to thoroughly mix the recipe.

Method

1. If your tripe is already minced, place it in the bowl. If not, grind or chop it before adding it to the bowl.

2. Chop the chicken meat into bite-sized chunks and add to bowl

3. Twist the heads off the sardines and add them whole. Grind or chop the fish bodies along with the oysters and beef liver. Add to bowl.

4. Divide the mixture into one or multiple roasting tins, crockery pots, or casserole dishes, and slow cook in the oven at 212F/100C for 3 to 4 hours.

5. Once the meat & fish mix is cooked, allow it to cool, and then use your hands to crumble the mix back into the bowl.

6. Chop the sunflower seeds and add to the mix

7. Grind the poppy seeds and flax/chia seeds and add them to the mix

8. Now add all the dry powdered ingredients: turmeric, bonemeal, yeast, salt & kelp

9. Thoroughly mix the entire recipe

10. Weigh out a suitably sized portion to serve to your puppy.

For the best long-term health, practice body condition scoring, use the growth charts, and try not to over- or underfeed. Refrigerate or freeze the remainder.

See Chapt. 5 for growth charts and portion sizing, Chapt. 6 for substitutions, Chapts. 8-10 for additional method details, tips, & advice, Chapt. 11 for storage info. and Chapt. 12 for online suppliers.

Nutritional Information

MACRONUTRIENT ANALYSIS			
Composition	As formulated	Dry Matter	% kcal
Protein	17.74%	59.65%	50.85%
Fat	6.20%	20.86%	43.19%
Ash	2.45%	8.24%	
Moisture	70.27%		
Fiber	1.26%	4.25%	
Net Carbs	2.08%	6.99%	5.95%
Sugars	0.32%	1.07%	0.91%
Starch	1.15%	3.87%	3.3%
Total			100%

MACRONUTRIENT INFORMATION

Total kcal in recipe	10,000
kcal / oz	35
kcal / lb	554
kcal / 100g	122
kcal / kg	1,221

MINERALS

	Unit	Min	Max	Recipe
Ca	g	2.5	5	3.33
P	g	2.25		3.02
Ca:P	ratio	1:1	1.8:1	1.10 : 1
K	g	1.1		2.28
Na	g	0.55		1.14
MG	g	0.1		0.4
Cl	g	0.83		0.84
Fe	mg	22	350	26.36
Cu	mg	2.75	7	3.04
Mn	mg	1.4	40	17.31
Zn	mg	25	70	25.39
I	mg	0.38	3	0.53
Se	mg	0.1		0.13

VITAMINS

	Unit	Min	Max	Recipe
Vit A	IU	1,250		2,888.18
Vit C	mg			2.66
Vit D	IU	138		237.39
Vit E	IU	12.5		12.98
Thiamine, B1	mg	0.45		1.47
Riboflavine, B2	mg	1.05		2.79
Niacin, B3	mg	3.4		46.76
Pantothenic Acid, B5	mg	3		5.55
B6 (Pyridoxine)	mg	0.3		1.56
Vit B12	mg	0.01		0.02
Folic Acid	mg	0.05		0.2
Choline	mg	425		610.55
Vit K1	mg			0
Biotin	mg			0.1

FATS				
	Unit	Min	Max	Recipe
Total	g	21.25		50.82
Saturated	g			16.3
Monounsaturated	g			15.18
Polyunsaturated	g			16.61
LA	g	3.25	16.25	12.18
ALA	g	0.2		1.47
AA	g	0.08		0.48
EPA	g			0.53
DPA	g			0.13
DHA	g			0.65
Omega-6/Omega-3	ratio			4.57 : 1
EPA + DHA	g	0.13		1.18

AMINO ACIDS				
	Unit	Min	Max	Recipe
Total protein	g	62.5		145.29
Tryptophan	g	0.58		1.43
Threonine	g	2.03		4.97
Isoleucine	g	1.63		5.86
Leucine	g	3.23		9.31
Lysine*	g	2.2	7*	9.8
Methionine	g	0.88		3.47
M - Cystine	g	1.75		6.75
Phenylalanine	g	1.63		5.01
P - Tyrosine	g	3.25		11.67
Valine	g	1.7		6.08
Arginine	g	2.05		8.16
Histidine	g	0.98		3.99
Purines	mg			531.98
Taurine	g			0.12

NB kcal per weight values will vary according to cooking or if raw. The values given are based on cooked as per the recipe.

Holly's Hog

& Walnuts

As this recipe contains wild boar, there is a small but genuine risk of trichinella parasites. For this reason, we recommend cooking this recipe to eliminate the risk of infection. This recipe is balanced with the hog meat roasted until thoroughly cooked.

Formulated to AAFCO.

Ingredients

4,506g Wild boar

133g Mushrooms, brown, Italian, or crimini

686g Oysters

271g Beef liver

1,383g Oily fish

256g Carrots

233g Walnuts, black

123g Bonemeal

29g Kelp

13g Salt

2,450mg Choline e.g. 7 capsules at 350mg/cap

198mg Iron, e.g. 11 capsules at 18mg/cap

30g Cod liver oil

Please weigh all ingredients accurately.

You will need a large mixing bowl, tub, or small bucket and a large, sturdy, long-handled spoon to thoroughly mix the recipe.

Method – cooking is recommended with pork, hog, or boar

1. Chop about half the boar into bite-sized chunks and grind or finely chop the rest with the liver, oysters, and mushrooms. Place all into the mixing bowl.

2. Chop the oily fish into bite-sized chunks, preferably leaving the heads whole according to puppy size, and add to bowl.

3. Divide the mixture into one or multiple roasting tins, crockery pots, or casserole dishes and slow cook in the oven at 212F/100C for 3 to 4 hours until the juices run clear. It will smell good enough to eat!

4. Once the meat & fish mix is cooked, allow it to cool, and then use your hands to crumble the mix back into the bowl.

5. Chop & steam the carrots until just tender and add to bowl

6. Now add all the dry powdered ingredients: bonemeal, kelp & salt

7. Twist open any supplement capsules and sprinkle the powder into the bowl

8. Roughly mix everything until no dry powders are visible

9. Add the cod liver oil, then thoroughly mix the entire recipe

10. Weigh out a suitably sized portion to serve to your puppy.

For the best long-term health, practice body condition scoring, use the growth charts, and try not to over- or underfeed. Refrigerate or freeze the remainder.

See Chapt. 5 for growth charts and portion sizing, Chapt. 6 for substitutions, Chapts. 8-10 for additional method details, tips, & advice, Chapt. 11 for storage info. and Chapt. 12 for online suppliers.

Nutritional Information

MACRONUTRIENT ANALYSIS			
Composition	As formulated	Dry Matter	% kcal
Protein	22.8%	58.57%	51.72%
Fat	6.86%	17.63%	37.81%
Ash	3.42%	8.8%	
Moisture	61.08%		
Fiber	1.22%	3.15%	
Net Carbs	4.62%	11.86%	10.47%
Sugars	2.15%	5.52%	4.87%
Starch	0.89%	2.28%	2.02%
Total			100%

MACRONUTRIENT INFORMATION				
Total kcal in recipe				10,000
kcal / oz				44
kcal / lb				700
kcal / 100g				154
kcal / kg				1.543

MINERALS				
	Unit	Min	Max	Recipe
Ca	g	3	4.5	4.14
P	g	2.5	4	3.03
Ca:P	ratio	1:1	2:1	1.37 : 1
K	g	1.5		1.54
Na	g	0.8		1
MG	g	0.15		0.17
Cl	g	1.1		1.31
Fe	mg	22		27.91
Cu	mg	3.1		5.17
Mn	mg	1.8		1.82
Zn	mg	25		28.5
I	mg	0.25	2.75	1.93
Se	mg	0.09		0.14

VITAMINS				
	Unit	Min	Max	Recipe
Vit A	IU	1,250	62,500	22,698.37
Vit C	mg			6.89
Vit D	IU	125	750	553.43
Vit E	IU	12.5		12.99
Thiamine, B1	mg	0.56		1.06
Riboflavine, B2	mg	1.3		1.62
Niacin, B3	mg	3.4		28.58
Pantothenic Acid, B5	mg	3		3.42
B6 (Pyridoxine)	mg	0.38		0.49
Vit B12	mg	0.01		0.02
Folic Acid	mg	0.05		0.11
Choline	mg	340		373.84
Vit K1	mg			0.01
Biotin	mg			0.24

FATS				
	Unit	Min	Max	Recipe
Total	g	21.3		44.49
Saturated	g			9.17
Monounsaturated	g			14.82
Polyunsaturated	g			14.58
LA	g	3.3		9.59
ALA	g	0.2		0.82
AA	g	0.08		0.55
EPA	g			0.85
DPA	g			0.14
DHA	g			1.22
Omega-6/Omega-3	ratio		30:1	2.99 : 1
EPA + DHA	g	0.1		2.07

AMINO ACIDS				
	Unit	Min	Max	Recipe
Total protein	g	56.3		147.76
Tryptophan	g	0.5		1.89
Threonine	g	2.6		6.51
Isoleucine	g	1.78		6.91
Leucine	g	3.23		11.75
Lysine*	g	2.25		13.46
Methionine	g	0.88		3.69
M - Cystine	g	1.75		5.57
Phenylalanine	g	2.08		5.9
P - Tyrosine	g	3.25		11
Valine	g	1.7		7.74
Arginine	g	2.5		10.25
Histidine	g	1.1		6.26
Purines	mg			438.27
Taurine	g			0.23

NB kcal per weight values will vary according to cooking or if raw. The values given are based on cooked as per the recipe.

Poppy's Caribou
& Hazlenuts

Poppy was dumped in the woods opposite our house. We found her curled up in one of the dog beds in our conservatory. We expected someone to claim her and put up posters, but she had clearly been deserted and was here to stay. She was a hunter through and through, although rabbits rather than caribou were her favored quarry!

Formulated to FEDIAF

Ingredients

4,507g Caribou

2,138g Salmon

578g Spinach

335g Oysters

173g Hazlenuts or filberts

113g Poppy seeds

62g Bonemeal

58g Basil, dried

11g Salt

9g Kelp powder (I = 700mcg/g)

5,250mg Choline, typically 15 capsules at 350mg/cap

18g Cod liver oil

Please weigh all ingredients accurately.

You will need a large mixing bowl, tub, or small bucket and a large, sturdy, long-handled spoon to thoroughly mix the recipe.

Method – cooking is optional

1. Chop about half the caribou and salmon into bite-sized chunks, and grind or finely chop the rest, along with the oysters. Place all the ingredients into the mixing bowl.

2. Divide the mixture into one or multiple roasting tins, crockery pots, or casserole dishes and slow cook in the oven at

212F/100C for 3 to 4 hours until the juices run clear.

3. Once the meat & fish mix is cooked, allow it to cool, and then use your hands to crumble the mix back into the bowl.

4. Chop the spinach and steam to wilt, then add to the mix

5. Chop the nuts and grind the seeds, then add those to the bowl

6. Now add all the dry powdered ingredients: bonemeal, basil, salt & kelp

7. Twist open supplement capsules and sprinkle the powder into the bowl

8. Roughly mix everything until no dry powders are visible

9. Add the cod liver oil, then thoroughly mix the entire recipe

10. Weigh out a suitably sized portion to serve to your puppy.

For the best long-term health, practice body condition scoring, use the growth charts, and try not to over- or underfeed. Refrigerate or freeze the remainder.

See Chapt. 5 for growth charts and portion sizing, Chapt. 6 for substitutions, Chapts. 8-10 for additional method details, tips, & advice, Chapt. 11 for storage info. and Chapt. 12 for online suppliers.

Nutritional Information

MACRONUTRIENT ANALYSIS			
Composition	As formulated	Dry Matter	% kcal
Protein	20.15%	65.26%	56.55%
Fat	5.73%	18.55%	39.04%
Ash	2.49%	8.08%	
Moisture	69.12%		
Fiber	0.93%	3.01%	
Net Carbs	1.57%	5.1%	4.42%
Sugars	0.18%	0.59%	0.51%
Starch	0.36%	1.17%	1.01%
Total			100%

MACRONUTRIENT INFORMATION				
Total kcal in recipe				10,000
kcal / oz				35
kcal / lb				566
kcal / 100g				125
kcal / kg				1,247

MINERALS				
	Unit	Min	Max	Recipe
Ca	g	2.5	5	2.94
P	g	2.25		2.81
Ca:P	ratio	1:1	1.8:1	1.05 : 1
K	g	1.1		2.82
Na	g	0.55		0.99
MG	g	0.1		0.35
Cl	g	0.83		0.98
Fe	mg	22	350	34.09
Cu	mg	2.75	7	2.75
Mn	mg	1.4	40	3.48
Zn	mg	25	70	34.36
I	mg	0.38	3	0.71
Se	mg	0.1		0.14

VITAMINS				
	Unit	Min	Max	Recipe
Vit A	IU	1,250		4,775.38
Vit C	mg			14.04
Vit D	IU	138		1,347.62
Vit E	IU	12.5		12.59
Thiamine, B1	mg	0.45		1.08
Riboflavine, B2	mg	1.05		3.73
Niacin, B3	mg	3.4		37.81
Pantothenic Acid, B5	mg	3		11.81
B6 (Pyridoxine)	mg	0.3		1.32
Vit B12	mg	0.01		0.03
Folic Acid	mg	0.05		0.14
Choline	mg	425		488.92
Vit K1	mg			0.26
Biotin	mg			0.13

FATS				
	Unit	Min	Max	Recipe
Total	g	21.25		45.92
Saturated	g			10.76
Monounsaturated	g			18.22
Polyunsaturated	g			11.46
LA	g	3.25	16.25	5.58
ALA	g	0.2		0.39
AA	g	0.08		0.7
EPA	g			1.33
DPA	g			0.33
DHA	g			2.16
Omega-6/Omega-3	ratio			1.67 : 1
EPA + DHA	g	0.13		3.49

AMINO ACIDS				
	Unit	Min	Max	Recipe
Total protein	g	62.5		161.57
Tryptophan	g	0.58		2.24
Threonine	g	2.03		7.07
Isoleucine	g	1.63		7.32
Leucine	g	3.23		12.81
Lysine*	g	2.2	7*	14.1
Methionine	g	0.88		3.89
M - Cystine	g	1.75		5.21
Phenylalanine	g	1.63		6.95
P - Tyrosine	g	3.25		12.36
Valine	g	1.7		7.9
Arginine	g	2.05		10.05
Histidine	g	0.98		5.63
Purines	mg			377.31
Taurine	g			0.26

NB kcal per weight values will vary according to cooking or if raw. The values given are based on cooked as per the recipe.

LOW PURINE. Puppies from 50% to 80% adult weight

Likely from 14 to 16 weeks old.

These balanced, low-purine recipes are suitable for Dalmatians (HUA) and other puppies with hyperuricosuria. They are also entirely suitable and balanced for other puppies, but puppies (and adult dogs) with hyperuricosuria must ONLY be fed from the low-purine recipe ranges in each section.

They include a range of raw and cooked options. These contain more supplementation by necessity, as the necessary nutrient balance for puppies cannot readily be achieved solely through whole foods containing no organ meat, oily fish, oysters, or other high-purine ingredients.

Puzzle's Fish

& Cottage Cheese

Finding a wide range of low-purine ingredients can be challenging, and purine data is not always available. If the data is missing, it is important to be cautious and stick with foods for which purine content is known to be low. Tripe, fish, and cottage cheese are firm favorites, but they are not enough on their own. Other nutrients must be added.

Formulated to FEDIAF. Balanced RAW

Ingredients

5,770g Whitefish

2,885g Beef tripe

1,118g Cottage cheese, full-fat

894g Carrots

224g Almonds

112g Sunflower seeds

95g Turmeric

90g Bonemeal

5g Kelp powder (I = 700mcg/g)

180mg Zinc, e.g. 12 capsules at 15mg/cap

54mg Iron, e.g. 3 capsules at 18mg/cap

30mg Copper, e.g. 15 capsules at 2mg/cap

Please weigh all ingredients accurately.

You will need a large mixing bowl, tub, or small bucket and a large, sturdy, long-handled spoon to thoroughly mix the recipe.

Method

1. Chop roughly half the whitefish, tripe into bite-sized chunks, and grind the rest. If your tripe is already ground, simply chop more of the fish into chunks to end up with a roughly 50:50 mix. Add to the bowl.

2. Put the cottage cheese straight into the bowl with the tripe and fish

3. You can grate the carrots or, preferably, juice them, adding pulp and juice to the mix.

4. Chop the almonds and grind the sunflower seeds before adding to the bowl

5. Now add all the dry powdered ingredients: spirulina, turmeric, bonemeal, salt & kelp

6. Twist open any supplement capsules and sprinkle the powder into the bowl

7. Thoroughly mix the entire recipe

8. Weigh out a suitably sized portion to serve to your puppy.

For the best long-term health, practice body condition scoring, use the growth charts, and try not to over- or underfeed. Refrigerate or freeze the remainder.

See Chapt. 5 for growth charts and portion sizing, Chapt. 6 for substitutions, Chapts. 8-10 for additional method details, tips, & advice, Chapt. 11 for storage info. and Chapt. 12 for online suppliers.

Nutritional Information

MACRONUTRIENT ANALYSIS			
Composition	As formulated	Dry Matter	% kcal
Protein	14.26%	62.6%	56%
Fat	3.86%	16.95%	36.83%
Ash	2.06%	9.06%	
Moisture	77.22%		
Fiber	0.77%	3.37%	
Net Carbs	1.83%	8.02%	7.18%
Sugars	0.88%	3.86%	3.46%
Starch	0.77%	3.38%	3.03%
Total			100%

MACRONUTRIENT INFORMATION			
Total kcal in recipe			10,000
kcal / oz			25
kcal / lb			404
kcal / 100g			891
kcal / kg			3913

MINERALS				
	Unit	Min	Max	Recipe
Ca	g	2.5	5	3.36
P	g	2.25		3.3
Ca:P	ratio	1:1	1.8:1	1.02 : 1
K	g	1.1		3.06
Na	g	0.55		1.33
MG	g	0.1		0.36
Cl	g	0.83		1.01
Fe	mg	22	350	22.02
Cu	mg	2.75	7	4.11
Mn	mg	1.4	40	3.19
Zn	mg	25	70	26.82
I	mg	0.38	3	0.5
Se	mg	0.1		0.23

VITAMINS				
	Unit	Min	Max	Recipe
Vit A	IU	1,250		14,147.30
Vit C	mg			4.7
Vit D	IU	138		753.41
Vit E	IU	12.5		19.01
Thiamine, B1	mg	0.45		0.75
Riboflavine, B2	mg	1.05		1.09
Niacin, B3	mg	3.4		22.07
Pantothenic Acid, B5	mg	3		4.51
B6 (Pyridoxine)	mg	0.3		1.57
Vit B12	mg	0.01		0.01
Folic Acid	mg	0.05		0.14
Choline	mg	425		964.88
Vit K1	mg			0.01
Biotin	mg			0.31

FATS				
	Unit	Min	Max	Recipe
Total	g	21.25		43.33
Saturated	g			10.01
Monounsaturated	g			16.76
Polyunsaturated	g			10.01
LA	g	3.25	16.25	6.33
ALA	g	0.2		0.34
AA	g	0.08		0.37
EPA	g			0.68
DPA	g			0.03
DHA	g			1.6
Omega-6/Omega-3	ratio			2.64 : 1
EPA + DHA	g	0.13		2.27

AMINO ACIDS				
	Unit	Min	Max	Recipe
Total protein	g	62.5		159.99
Tryptophan	g	0.58		1.82
Threonine	g	2.03		6.74
Isoleucine	g	1.63		7.27
Leucine	g	3.23		12.84
Lysine*	g	2.2	7*	13.64
Methionine	g	0.88		4.64
M - Cystine	g	1.75		6.38
Phenylalanine	g	1.63		6.54
P - Tyrosine	g	3.25		12.17
Valine	g	1.7		8.12
Arginine	g	2.05		10.13
Histidine	g	0.98		4.7
Purines	mg			754.83
Taurine	g			0.61

NB kcal per weight values will vary according to cooking or if raw. The following values are based on lightly cooked.

Vesper Chicken

& Creamy Chickpeas

We took puppy Vesper to the airport for export, and the entire plane was a puppy delivery service. There were puppies of all types and sizes. The co-pilot was super friendly, talking with each pup as they were loaded. Vesper is now a champion detection dog and travels widely, displaying and teaching her skills.

Formulated to FEDIAF. Balanced RAW or COOKED

Ingredients

2,997g Chicken meat excl. skin and bones

1,001g Fish roe, herring, or salmon. Avoid pollock.

468g Yogurt, plain whole milk

375g Egg, whole, no shell

332g Chickpeas, garbanzo beans, canned or cooked

38g Carrot

222g Peanuts, shelled

81g Bonemeal

61g Turmeric

47g Spirulina

33g Oregano

7g Salt

7g Kelp (I = 700mcg/g)

180mg Zinc, e.g. 12 capsules at 15mg/cap

108mg Iron, e.g. 6 capsules at 18mg/cap

20mg Copper, e.g. 10 capsules at 2mg/cap

24g Cod liver oil

Please weigh all ingredients accurately.

You will need a large mixing bowl, tub, or small bucket and a large, sturdy, long-handled spoon to thoroughly mix the recipe.

Method – cooking is optional

1. Chop the chicken into bite-sized chunks and add to bowl

2. Break up or mash the roe into the bowl

3. Divide the mixture into one or multiple roasting tins, crockery pots, or casserole dishes, and slow cook in the oven at 212F/100C for 3 to 4 hours until cooked.

4. Once the meat & roe mix is cooked, allow to cool, and then use your hands to crumble the mix back into the bowl.

5. Add the yogurt, eggs, and chickpeas.

6. Grate the carrot straight into the bowl—it may not seem much, but it adds vitamin A. Don't bulk out with extra carrot, or you'll dilute other mineral quantities.

7. Chop the peanuts and add to the mix.

8. Now add all the dry powdered ingredients: bonemeal, turmeric, spirulina, oregano, salt & kelp.

9. Twist open any supplement capsules and sprinkle the powder into the bowl

10. Roughly mix everything until no dry powders are visible

11. Add the cod liver oil, then thoroughly mix the entire recipe

12. Weigh out a suitably sized portion to serve to your puppy.

For the best long-term health, practice body condition scoring, use the growth charts, and try not to over- or underfeed. Refrigerate or freeze the remainder.

See Chapt. 5 for growth charts and portion sizing, Chapt. 6 for substitutions, Chapts. 8-10 for additional method details, tips, & advice, Chapt. 11 for storage info. and Chapt. 12 for online suppliers.

Nutritional Information

MACRONUTRIENT ANALYSIS

Composition		As formulated	Dry Matter	% kcal
Protein		17.02%	47.16%	34.08%
Fat		12.42%	34.42%	60.41%
Ash		2.73%	7.57%	
Moisture		63.91%		
Fiber		1.16%	3.23%	
Net Carbs		2.75%	7.62%	5.51%
Sugars		0.72%	2.01%	1.45%
Starch		0.49%	1.36%	0.99%
Total				100%

MACRONUTRIENT INFORMATION

Total kcal in recipe				10,000
kcal / oz				50
kcal / lb				793
kcal / 100g				175
kcal / kg				1,748

MINERALS

	Unit	Min	Max	Recipe
Ca	g	2.5	5	2.8
P	g	2.25		2.32
Ca:P	ratio	1:1	1.8:1	1.21:1
K	g	1.1		1.49
Na	g	0.55		0.88
MG	g	0.1		0.18
Cl	g	0.83		0.88
Fe	mg	22	350	23.2
Cu	mg	2.75	7	2.88
Mn	mg	1.4	40	2.26
Zn	mg	25	70	26.41
I	mg	0.38	3	0.51
Se	mg	0.1		0.11

VITAMINS				
	Unit	Min	Max	Recipe
Vit A	IU	1,250		1,332.34
Vit C	mg			14.29
Vit D	IU	138		735.79
Vit E	IU	12.5		18.56
Thiamine, B1	mg	0.45		0.5
Riboflavine, B2	mg	1.05		1.7
Niacin, B3	mg	3.4		19.71
Pantothenic Acid, B5	mg	3		5.29
B6 (Pyridoxine)	mg	0.3		0.79
Vit B12	mg	0.01		0.01
Folic Acid	mg	0.05		0.15
Choline	mg	425		427.94
Vit K1	mg			0.02
Biotin	mg			0.14

FATS				
	Unit	Min	Max	Recipe
Total	g	21.25		71.07
Saturated	g			17.6
Monounsaturated	g			26.65
Polyunsaturated	g			17.92
LA	g	3.25	16.25	12.36
ALA	g	0.2		0.55
AA	g	0.08		1
EPA	g			1.24
DPA	g			0.22
DHA	g			1.79
Omega-6/Omega-3	ratio			3.81 : 1
EPA + DHA	g	0.13		3.03

AMINO ACIDS				
	Unit	Min	Max	Recipe
Total protein	g	62.5		97.38
Tryptophan	g	0.58		1.13
Threonine	g	2.03		4.23
Isoleucine	g	1.63		4.72
Leucine	g	3.23		7.84
Lysine*	g	2.2	7*	7.7
Methionine	g	0.88		2.46
M - Cystine	g	1.75		3.79
Phenylalanine	g	1.63		4.23
P - Tyrosine	g	3.25		8.04
Valine	g	1.7		5.05
Arginine	g	2.05		6.48
Histidine	g	0.98		2.71
Purines	mg			489.77
Taurine	g			0.54

NB kcal per weight values will vary according to cooking or if raw. The values given are based on cooked as per the recipe.

80% adult weight to maturity

Raw

These recipes have been balanced based on ingredients being left raw.

You can always 'step back' and feed recipes for the previous age group; don't jump forward to an older age group recipe.

Re-visit Chapter 5 for more information about different growth phases, growth charts, and how to score body condition.

Belle's Lamb

& Pumpkin

This recipe uses lamb heart, but if you don't readily find it, you can substitute beef heart. The nutritional balance remains unchanged, with just a slight increase of 11kcal for the recipe batch. Likewise, switching the turkey necks for duck necks is fine, but chicken necks are not a good swap as they have a lower mineral content.

Formulated to FEDIAF

Ingredients

3,660g Lamb 85% lean

366g Turkey necks with bone

292g Oysters

194g Beef liver

183g Beef spleen

146g Lamb heart

220g Egg. whole, no shell

220g Pumpkin

220g Leafy green veg

88g Almonds

110g Spirulina

62g Bonemeal

31g Turmeric

11g Cod liver oil

9g Salt

6g Kelp (I = 700mcg/g)

Please weigh all ingredients accurately.

This recipe requires a meat grinder that can cope with poultry bones.

You will need a large mixing bowl, tub, or small bucket and a large, sturdy, long-handled spoon to thoroughly mix the recipe.

Method

1. Chop roughly half the lamb into bite-sized chunks and grind the rest. Place in the bowl

2. Grind the turkey necks with the oysters, liver, spleen & heart. Add to the bowl.

3. Add the fresh eggs straight into the mix.

4. Juice the pumpkin and leafy greens and add juice and pulp to the mix. Alternatively, chop them finely.

5. Chop the almonds before adding them to the bowl.

6. Now add all the dry powdered ingredients: spirulina, bonemeal, turmeric, salt & kelp.

7. Thoroughly mix the entire recipe

8. Weigh out a suitably sized portion to serve to your puppy.

For the best long-term health, practice body condition scoring, use the growth charts, and try not to over- or underfeed. Refrigerate or freeze the remainder.

See Chapt. 5 for growth charts and portion sizing, Chapt. 6 for substitutions, Chapts. 8-10 for additional method details, tips, & advice, Chapt. 11 for storage info. and Chapt. 12 for online suppliers.

Nutritional Information

MACRONUTRIENT ANALYSIS			
Composition	As formulated	Dry Matter	% kcal
Protein	17.28%	51.12%	37.67%
Fat	12.15%	35.95%	59.61%
Ash	2.52%	7.44%	
Moisture	66.2%		
Fiber	0.61%	1.81%	
Net Carbs	1.25%	3.69%	2.72%
Sugars	0.5%	1.47%	1.08%
Starch	0.74%	2.18%	1.6%
Total			100%

MACRONUTRIENT INFORMATION				
Total kcal in recipe				10,000
kcal / oz				52
kcal / lb				832
kcal / 100g				183
kcal / kg				1,835

MINERALS				
	Unit	Min	Max	Recipe
Ca	g	2	5	1.96
P	g	1.75		1.75
Ca:P	ratio	1:1	1.6:1	1.12 : 1
K	g	1.1		1.61
Na	g	0.55		0.79
MG	g	0.1		0.19
Cl	g	0.83		0.99
Fe	mg	22	350	25.58
Cu	mg	2.75	7	3.64
Mn	mg	1.4	40	1.46
Zn	mg	25	70	25.04
I	mg	0.38	3	0.46
Se	mg	0.1		0.12

VITAMINS				
	Unit	Min	Max	Recipe
Vit A	IU	1,250		6,606.16
Vit C	mg			22.81
Vit D	IU	125		232.52
Vit E	IU	12.5		14.9
Thiamine, B1	mg	0.45		0.85
Riboflavine, B2	mg	1.05		2.18
Niacin, B3	mg	3.4		33.59
Pantothenic Acid, B5	mg	3		5.89
B6 (Pyridoxine)	mg	0.3		1.06
Vit B12	mg	0.01		0.03
Folic Acid	mg	0.05		0.2
Choline	mg	425		441.54
Vit K1	mg			0.09
Biotin	mg			0.31

FATS				
	Unit	Min	Max	Recipe
Total	g	21.25		66.23
Saturated	g			27.3
Monounsaturated	g			24.8
Polyunsaturated	g			6.72
LA	g	3.25	16.25	5.06
ALA	g	0.2		0.88
AA	g	0.08		0.24
EPA	g			0.26
DPA	g			0.1
DHA	g			0.2
Omega-6/Omega-3	ratio			3.75 : 1
EPA + DHA	g	0.13		0.45

AMINO ACIDS				
	Unit	Min	Max	Recipe
Total protein	g	50		94.18
Tryptophan	g	0.53		1.1
Threonine	g	1.6		4.15
Isoleucine	g	1.25		4.33
Leucine	g	2		7.42
Lysine*	g	1.75	7*	7.78
Methionine	g	0.65		2.39
M - Cystine	g	1.33		3.53
Phenylalanine	g	1.25		4.07
P - Tyrosine	g	2.5		7.41
Valine	g	1.4		4.79
Arginine	g	1.73		5.87
Histidine	g	0.63		2.61
Purines	mg			588.89
Taurine	g			0.14

NB kcal per weight values will vary according to cooking or if raw. The following values are based on lightly cooked.

Lottie's Surprise
With Spirulina

Lottie is one of our water-loving puppies. Her owner keeps in touch with fabulous photos of Lottie mud-sliding in wet pasture land and even jumping into water troughs and ponds. She loves getting wet and muddy, the original definition of a mucky pup!

Formulated to FEDIAF

Ingredients

1,112g Chicken legs with skin and bone

209g Chicken gizzards

246g Beef liver

209g Beef kidney

361g Oysters

1,390g Oily fish

1,390g Beef tripe

1,390g Rabbit meat

296g Blueberries

160g Hempseed

104g Spirulina

70g Bonemeal

7g Kelp (I = 700mcg/g)

7g Salt

20g Cod liver oil

Please weigh all ingredients accurately.

This recipe requires a meat grinder/mincer that can cope with poultry bones.

You will need a large mixing bowl, tub, or small bucket and a large, sturdy, long-handled spoon to thoroughly mix the recipe.

Method

1. Grind together the chicken legs, gizzards, liver, kidney and oysters

2. Twist the heads off the fish and add whole, or if they seem too big for your pup, you might cut them into bite-sized chunks

3. Now look at the bowl of grind and all the fish & meat you have left. Grind or chop into bite-sized chunks as necessary to end up with an approx. 50:50 mix of grind and chunks.

4. Add the blueberries

5. Grind the hempseed and add to the mix

6. Now add all the dry powdered ingredients: spirulina, bonemeal, kelp & salt

7. Roughly mix everything until no dry powders are visible

8. Add the cod liver oil, then thoroughly mix the entire recipe

9. Weigh out a suitably sized portion to serve to your puppy.

For the best long-term health, practice body condition scoring, use the growth charts, and try not to over- or underfeed. Refrigerate or freeze the remainder.

See Chapt. 5 for growth charts and portion sizing, Chapt. 6 for substitutions, Chapts. 8-10 for additional method details, tips, & advice, Chapt. 11 for storage info. and Chapt. 12 for online suppliers.

Nutritional Information

MACRONUTRIENT ANALYSIS			
Composition	As formulated	Dry Matter	% kcal
Protein	19.16%	63%	53.42%
Fat	6.81%	22.38%	42.7%
Ash	2.7%	8.87%	
Moisture	69.59%		
Fiber	0.35%	1.16%	
Net Carbs	1.39%	4.58%	3.89%
Sugars	0.68%	2.24%	1.9%
Starch	0.46%	1.51%	1.28%
Total			100%

MACRONUTRIENT INFORMATION					
Total kcal in recipe					10,000
kcal / oz					41
kcal / lb					651
kcal / 100g					143
kcal / kg					1,435

MINERALS				
	Unit	Min	Max	Recipe
Ca	g	2	5	3.6
P	g	1.75		3.07
Ca:P	ratio	1:1	1.6:1	1.17 : 1
K	g	1.1		2.21
Na	g	0.55		0.93
MG	g	0.1		0.36
Cl	g	0.83		1.06
Fe	mg	22	350	22.29
Cu	mg	2.75	7	2.97
Mn	mg	1.4	40	2.03
Zn	mg	25	70	25.02
I	mg	0.38	3	0.57
Se	mg	0.1		0.17

VITAMINS				
	Unit	Min	Max	Recipe
Vit A	IU	1,250		4,940.51
Vit C	mg			6.19
Vit D	IU	125		630.42
Vit E	IU	12.5		13.18
Thiamine, B1	mg	0.45		1.05
Riboflavine, B2	mg	1.05		2.53
Niacin, B3	mg	3.4		39.95
Pantothenic Acid, B5	mg	3		8.47
B6 (Pyridoxine)	mg	0.3		2.43
Vit B12	mg	0.01		0.05
Folic Acid	mg	0.05		0.18
Choline	mg	425		657.98
Vit K1	mg			0.01
Biotin	mg			0.18

FATS				
	Unit	Min	Max	Recipe
Total	g	21.25		47.44
Saturated	g			12.41
Monounsaturated	g			15.17
Polyunsaturated	g			14.37
LA	g	3.25	16.25	8.35
ALA	g	0.2		1.93
AA	g	0.08		0.36
EPA	g			0.9
DPA	g			0.21
DHA	g			1.38
Omega-6/Omega-3	ratio			2.01 : 1
EPA + DHA	g	0.13		2.29

AMINO ACIDS				
	Unit	Min	Max	Recipe
Total protein	g	50		133.54
Tryptophan	g	0.53		1.59
Threonine	g	1.6		5.64
Isoleucine	g	1.25		6.25
Leucine	g	2		10.38
Lysine*	g	1.75	7*	10.91
Methionine	g	0.65		3.67
M - Cystine	g	1.33		5.36
Phenylalanine	g	1.25		5.47
P - Tyrosine	g	2.5		10.15
Valine	g	1.4		6.75
Arginine	g	1.73		8.87
Histidine	g	0.63		3.89
Purines	mg			864.02
Taurine	g			0.35

NB kcal per weight values will vary according to cooking or if raw. These values are based on lightly cooked.

Reggie's Rabbit

& Turkey

Rabbit meat can be bought frozen online. If you hunt rabbits or buy them whole from a hunter, I would keep that as a treat for adult dogs because data is not available for the nutritional content of whole rabbits, including bones with or without skin. I am not saying a whole rabbit would be unhealthy, but for growing puppies, it is safer to know and balance mineral content.

Formulated to AAFCO

Ingredients

925g Chicken backs incl. bone

198g Beef spleen

185g Beef liver

2,765g Rabbit, 95% lean

925g Turkey meat, no skin

370g Eggs, whole, no shell

601g Sweet potato

370g Eggs, whole, no shell

93g Bonemeal

75g Turmeric

12g Salt

10g Nutritional yeast

6g Kelp

165mg Zinc, e.g. 11 capsules at 15mg/cap

18mg Copper, e.g. 9 capsules at 2mg/cap

22g Cod liver oil

Please weigh all ingredients accurately.

This recipe requires a meat grinder that can cope with poultry bones.

You will need a large mixing bowl, tub, or small bucket and a large, sturdy, long-handled spoon to thoroughly mix the recipe.

Method

1. Grind together the chicken backs, spleen, and liver and place in your bowl

2. Now look at the bowl of grind and all the rabbit & turkey meat you have. Grind or chop into bite-sized chunks to end up with an approx. 50:50 mix of grind and chunks.

3. Juice the sweet potato, adding pulp and juice into the bowl, or grate it before adding.

4. Add the eggs

5. Now add all the dry powdered ingredients: bonemeal, turmeric, salt, yeast & kelp.

6. Twist open any supplement capsules and sprinkle the powder into the bowl

7. Roughly mix everything until no dry powders are visible

8. Add the cod liver oil, then thoroughly mix the entire recipe

9. Weigh out a suitably sized portion to serve to your puppy.

For the best long-term health, practice body condition scoring, use the growth charts, and try not to over- or underfeed. Refrigerate or freeze the remainder.

See Chapt. 5 for growth charts and portion sizing, Chapt. 6 for substitutions, Chapts. 8-10 for additional method details, tips, & advice, Chapt. 11 for storage info. and Chapt. 12 for online suppliers.

Nutritional Information

MACRONUTRIENT ANALYSIS			
Composition	As formulated	Dry Matter	% kcal
Protein	20.33%	59.68%	50.46%
Fat	7.79%	22.88%	43.51%
Ash	2.9%	8.51%	
Moisture	65.94%		
Fiber	0.61%	1.8%	
Net Carbs	2.43%	7.13%	6.03%
Sugars	0.65%	1.89%	1.6%
Starch	1.85%	5.43%	4.59%
Total			100%

MACRONUTRIENT INFORMATION				
Total kcal in recipe				10,000
kcal / oz				46
kcal / lb				731
kcal / 100g				161
kcal / kg				1,612

MINERALS				
	Unit	Min	Max	Recipe
Ca	g	3	4.5	3.38
P	g	2.5	4	2.81
Ca:P	ratio	1:1	2:1	1.20 : 1
K	g	1.5		2.26
Na	g	0.8		0.92
MG	g	0.15		0.31
Cl	g	1.1		1.17
Fe	mg	22		25.38
Cu	mg	3.1		3.21
Mn	mg	1.8		1.84
Zn	mg	25		26.7
I	mg	0.25	2.75	0.45
Se	mg	0.09		0.12

VITAMINS				
	Unit	Min	Max	Recipe
Vit A	IU	1,250	62,500	12,370.30
Vit C	mg			12.29
Vit D	IU	125	750	416.09
Vit E	IU	12.5		13.04
Thiamine, B1	mg	0.56		1.15
Riboflavine, B2	mg	1.3		2.07
Niacin, B3	mg	3.4		47.77
Pantothenic Acid, B5	mg	3		8.02
B6 (Pyridoxine)	mg	0.38		3.82
Vit B12	mg	0.01		0.04
Folic Acid	mg	0.05		0.21
Choline	mg	340		432.81
Vit K1	mg			0.01
Biotin	mg			0.18

FATS				
	Unit	Min	Max	Recipe
Total	g	21.3		48.35
Saturated	g			14.36
Monounsaturated	g			18.3
Polyunsaturated	g			9.88
LA	g	3.3		7.72
ALA	g	0.2		0.74
AA	g			0.2
EPA	g			0.2
DPA	g			0.05
DHA	g			0.26
Omega-6/Omega-3	ratio		30:1	6.23:1
EPA+DHA	g	0.1		0.46

AMINO ACIDS				
	Unit	Min	Max	Recipe
Total protein	g	56.3		126.14
Tryptophan	g	0.5		1.59
Threonine	g	2.6		5.39
Isoleucine	g	1.78		5.62
Leucine	g	3.23		9.66
Lysine*	g	2.25		10.57
Methionine	g	0.88		3.12
M - Cystine	g	1.75		4.77
Phenylalanine	g	2.08		5.08
P - Tyrosine	g	3.25		9.38
Valine	g	1.7		6.18
Arginine	g	2.5		7.67
Histidine	g	1.1		3.5
Purines	mg			633.93
Taurine	g			0.1

*NB kcal per weight values will vary according to cooking or if raw. The following values are based on lightly cooked.

Siam's Goat

& Gizzards

Oily fish, usually mackerel, pilchards, sardines, etc., are often sold whole, frozen, online in 1 kg bags. You can weigh them out frozen so you don't defrost more than required for a batch at a time. We often have several different bags open to dip into for a recipe mix.

Formulated to FEDIAF

Ingredients

826g Turkey necks (or duck)

362g Chicken gizzards

151g Beef liver

124g Beef kidney

232g Oysters

1,033g Oily fish

3,098g Goat meat

310g Egg, whole, no shell

413g Edemame beans, canned or frozen, prepared

207g Apples with skin and core

155g Hempseed

124g Turmeric

62g Bonemeal

9g Salt

6g Kelp (I = 700mcg/g)

1,050mg Choline, e.g. 3 capsules at 350mg./cap

4g Cod liver oil

Please weigh all ingredients accurately.

This recipe requires a meat grinder that can cope with poultry bones.

You will need a large mixing bowl, tub, or small bucket and a large, sturdy, long-handled spoon to thoroughly mix the recipe.

Method

1. Grind together the chicken necks, gizzards, liver, kidney and oysters

2. Twist the heads off the fish and add whole, or if they seem too big for your pup, you might cut them into bite-sized chunks

3. Now look at the bowl of grind and all the fish & meat you have left. Grind or chop into bite-sized chunks to end up with an approx. 50:50 mix of grind and chunks.

4. Add the eggs to the bowl.

5. Mash the beans roughly and add them to the bowl.

6. Juice the apples and add both juice & fruit to the mix. Alternatively, you can grate the apples.

7. Grind the hempseed and add to the mix

8. Now add all the dry powdered ingredients: turmeric, bonemeal, salt & kelp

9. Twist open any supplement capsules and sprinkle the powder into the bowl

10. Roughly mix everything until no dry powders are visible

11. Add the cod liver oil, then thoroughly mix the entire recipe

12. Weigh out a suitably sized portion to serve to your puppy.

For the best long-term health, practice body condition scoring, use the growth charts, and try not to over- or underfeed. Refrigerate or freeze the remainder.

See Chapt. 5 for growth charts and portion sizing, Chapt. 6 for substitutions, Chapts. 8-10 for additional method details, tips, & advice, Chapt. 11 for storage info. and Chapt. 12 for online suppliers.

Nutritional Information

MACRONUTRIENT ANALYSIS

Composition		As formulated	Dry Matter	% kcal
Protein		18.29%	60.85%	52.07%
Fat		6.69%	22.27%	42.87%
Ash		2.44%	8.1%	
Moisture		69.94%		
Fiber		0.86%	2.87%	
Net Carbs		1.78%	5.91%	5.06%
Sugars		0.65%	2.16%	1.85%
Starch		1.1%	3.66%	3.13%
Total				100%

MACRONUTRIENT INFORMATION

Total kcal in recipe				10,000
kcal / oz				40
kcal / lb				637
kcal / 100g				141
kcal / kg				1,405

MINERALS

	Unit	Min	Max	Recipe
Ca	g	2	5	2.96
P	g	1.75		2.72
Ca:P	ratio	1:1	1.6:1	1.09:1
K	g	1.1		2.44
Na	g	0.55		0.87
MG	g	0.1		0.42
Cl	g	0.83		0.89
Fe	mg	22	350	23
Cu	mg	2.75	7	3.21
Mn	mg	1.4	40	4.41
Zn	mg	25	70	29.23
I	mg	0.38	3	0.46
Se	mg	0.1		0.13

VITAMINS				
	Unit	Min	Max	Recipe
Vit A	IU	1,250		3,334.62
Vit C	mg			6.68
Vit D	IU	125		393.2
Vit E	IU	12.5		12.75
Thiamine, B1	mg	0.45		0.91
Riboflavine, B2	mg	1.05		1.68
Niacin, B3	mg	3.4		27.3
Pantothenic Acid, B5	mg	3		4.88
B6 (Pyridoxine)	mg	0.3		1.12
Vit B12	mg	0.01		0.03
Folic Acid	mg	0.05		0.3
Choline	mg	425		425.46
Vit K1	mg			0.02
Biotin	mg			0.3

FATS				
	Unit	Min	Max	Recipe
Total	g	21.25		47.63
Saturated	g			15.46
Monounsaturated	g			14.43
Polyunsaturated	g			12.35
LA	g	3.25	16.25	7.49
ALA	g	0.2		1.74
AA	g	0.08		0.32
EPA	g			0.6
DPA	g			0.2
DHA	g			0.92
Omega-6/Omega-3	ratio			2.30 : 1
EPA + DHA	g	0.13		1.52

	Unit	Min	Max	Recipe
AMINO ACIDS				
Total protein	g	50		130.18
Tryptophan	g	0.53		1.29
Threonine	g	1.6		5.29
Isoleucine	g	1.25		5.47
Leucine	g	2		9.79
Lysine*	g	1.75	7*	10.37
Methionine	g	0.65		3.31
M - Cystine	g	1.33		4.12
Phenylalanine	g	1.25		5.12
P - Tyrosine	g	2.5		9.35
Valine	g	1.4		5.99
Arginine	g	1.73		8.93
Histidine	g	0.63		3.49
Purines	mg			436.96
Taurine	g			0.32

*NB kcal per weight values will vary according to cooking or if raw. The following values are based on lightly cooked.

Margo's Chicken
& Summer Squash

Margo was our only deaf Dalmatian puppy. Deafness is associated with white coat color, and a specific genetic connection has not been uncovered. She came to stay while her owners went away, and we took her camping with our dogs. We had the most wonderful time. Her grasp of sign language is nothing short of remarkable, and she frequently "checked in" when off-lead by looking over just in case we wanted to sign to her!

Formulated to FEDIAF

Ingredients

870g Chicken legs whole – including both bone & skin

387g Beef liver

155g Beef spleen

421g Oysters

2,900g Chicken legs or thighs incl. skin, excl. bone,

580g Beef tripe

174g Summer squash

174g Leafy greens

18g Brazil nuts

87g Sunflower seeds

87g Turmeric

44g bonemeal

7g Salt

5g Kelp

21g Cod liver oil

Please weigh all ingredients accurately.

This recipe requires a meat grinder that can cope with poultry bones.

You will need a large mixing bowl, tub, or small bucket and a large, sturdy, long-handled spoon to thoroughly mix the recipe.

Method

1. Grind together the chicken legs, liver, spleen, and oysters

2. Now look at the bowl of grind and all the tripe & chicken you have. Grind or chop into bite-sized chunks to end up with an approx. 50:50 mix of grind and chunks.

3. Juice the squash and greens, adding pulp and juice to the bowl. Alternatively, grate the squash and chop the greens before adding.

4. Chop the Barizl nuts, grind the sunflower seeds, and add both to the bowl

5. Now add all the dry powdered ingredients: turmeric, bonemeal, salt & kelp

6. Roughly mix everything until no dry powders are visible

7. Add the cod liver oil, then thoroughly mix the entire recipe

8. Weigh out a suitably sized portion to serve to your puppy.

For the best long-term health, practice body condition scoring, use the growth charts, and try not to over- or underfeed. Refrigerate or freeze the remainder.

See Chapt. 5 for growth charts and portion sizing, Chapt. 6 for substitutions, Chapts. 8-10 for additional method details, tips, & advice, Chapt. 11 for storage info. and Chapt. 12 for online suppliers.

Nutritional Information

MACRONUTRIENT ANALYSIS			
Composition	As formulated	Dry Matter	% kcal
Protein	15.27%	49.25%	36.21%
Fat	11.2%	36.1%	59.73%
Ash	2.23%	7.19%	
Moisture	68.99%		
Fiber	0.6%	1.94%	
Net Carbs	1.71%	5.51%	4.05%
Sugars	0.48%	1.53%	1.13%
Starch	1.18%	3.8%	2.8%
Total			100%

MACRONUTRIENT INFORMATION

Total kcal in recipe	10,000
kcal / oz	48
kcal / lb	765
kcal / 100g	169
kcal / kg	1,687

MINERALS

	Unit	Min	Max	Recipe
Ca	g	2	5	2.45
P	g	1.75		2.08
Ca:P	ratio	1:1	1.6:1	1.18 : 1
K	g	1.1		1.47
Na	g	0.55		0.78
MG	g	0.1		0.24
Cl	g	0.83		0.87
Fe	mg	22	350	22.68
Cu	mg	2.75	7	2.8
Mn	mg	1.4	40	2.72
Zn	mg	25	70	25.3
I	mg	0.38	3	0.39
Se	mg	0.1		0.15

VITAMINS

	Unit	Min	Max	Recipe
Vit A	IU	1,250		8,153.53
Vit C	mg			21.25
Vit D	IU	125		363.61
Vit E	IU	12.5		17.82
Thiamine, B1	mg	0.45		0.49
Riboflavine, B2	mg	1.05		1.91
Niacin, B3	mg	3.4		28.4
Pantothenic Acid, B5	mg	3		8.51
B6 (Pyridoxine)	mg	0.3		1.77
Vit B12	mg	0.01		0.03
Folic Acid	mg	0.05		0.21
Choline	mg	425		440.03
Vit K1	mg			0.08
Biotin	mg			0.19

FATS				
	Unit	Min	Max	Recipe
Total	g	21.25		66.37
Saturated	g			18.61
Monounsaturated	g			26.62
Polyunsaturated	g			15.07
LA	g	3.25	16.25	12.12
ALA	g	0.2		0.54
AA	g	0.08		0.48
EPA	g			0.35
DPA	g			0.09
DHA	g			0.37
Omega-6/Omega-3	ratio			9.76 : 1
EPA + DHA	g	0.13		0.72

AMINO ACIDS				
	Unit	Min	Max	Recipe
Total protein	g	50		90.54
Tryptophan	g	0.53		1.02
Threonine	g	1.6		3.77
Isoleucine	g	1.25		4.19
Leucine	g	2		7.13
Lysine*	g	1.75	7*	7.45
Methionine	g	0.65		2.43
M - Cystine	g	1.33		3.64
Phenylalanine	g	1.25		3.68
P - Tyrosine	g	2.5		6.79
Valine	g	1.4		4.5
Arginine	g	1.73		6.17
Histidine	g	0.63		2.65
Purines	mg			660.75
Taurine	g			0.56

*NB kcal per weight values will vary according to cooking or if raw. The following values are based on lightly cooked.

80% adult weight to maturity

Cooked or raw

These recipes have all been formulated and nutritionally balanced based upon light cooking or if left raw.

You can always 'step back' and feed recipes for the previous age group; don't jump forward to an older age group recipe.

In all recipes that might be cooked, we do not include natural sources of bone such as poultry wings, necks, and backs because cooked poultry bone can lead to sharp shards with potential internal injury or obstruction risks.

Olives Beef

& Broccoli

I realize oysters feature in many recipes, but they have such a helpful mineral content, particularly zinc, that it is tricky to balance a recipe without them unless we rely on supplements, but it's helpful to have choices. So if you don't have any oysters, then instead, you can add 30mg of zinc, e.g., 2 capsules at 15mg/cap, and increase the salt to 8g

Formulated to FEDIAF

Ingredients

2,827g Beef ground 90% lean

2,827g Beef tripe

318g Beef heart

226g Beef kidney

212g Salmon with bone

212g Oysters

212g Beef liver

600g Broccoli

85g Hempseed

78g Bonemeal

67g turmeric

36g Spirulina

7g Salt

7g Kelp (I = 700mcg/g)

4g Nutritional yeast

35g Cod liver oil

Please weigh all ingredients accurately.

You will need a large mixing bowl, tub, or small bucket and a large, sturdy, long-handled spoon to thoroughly mix the recipe.

Method – cooking is optional

1. Chop the tripe, heart, kidney, salmon, oysters, and liver into bite-sized chunks and place in a bowl with the ground beef. Mix evenly.

2. Divide the mixture into one or multiple roasting tins, crock pots, or casserole dishes and slow cook in the oven at 212F/100C for 2 to 3 hours until just cooked.

3. Allow to cool, and then use your hands to crumble the mix back into the bowl.

4. If you are leaving raw, finely chop or grind the kidney, oysters, and liver. Then, assess the remaining meat and chop or grind to end up with an approximate 50:50 chunk: ground meat mix.

5. Steam the broccoli until just tender, then chop and add to the bowl. If keeping raw, juice and add both pulp and juice to the bowl, or chop the florets and grate the stem.

6. Grind the hempseed and add to bowl.

7. Now add all the dry powdered ingredients: bonemeal, turmeric, spirulina, salt, kelp, & yeast.

8. Roughly mix everything until no dry powders are visible

9. Add the cod liver oil, then thoroughly mix the entire recipe

10. Weigh out a suitably sized portion to serve to your puppy.

For the best long-term health, practice body condition scoring, use the growth charts, and try not to over- or underfeed. Refrigerate or freeze the remainder.

See Chapt. 5 for growth charts and portion sizing, Chapt. 6 for substitutions, Chapts. 8-10 for additional method details, tips, & advice, Chapt. 11 for storage info. and Chapt. 12 for online suppliers.

Nutritional Information

MACRONUTRIENT ANALYSIS			
Composition	As formulated	Dry Matter	% kcal
Protein	15.71%	59.01%	48.73%
Fat	6.64%	24.95%	46.37%
Ash	2.19%	8.22%	
Moisture	73.37%		
Fiber	0.5%	1.89%	
Net Carbs	1.58%	5.93%	4.9%
Sugars	0.36%	1.37%	1.13%
Starch	0.61%	2.29%	1.89%
Total			100%

MACRONUTRIENT INFORMATION				
Total kcal in recipe				10,000
kcal / oz				37
kcal / lb				585
kcal / 100g				129
kcal / kg				1,290

MINERALS				
	Unit	Min	Max	Recipe
Ca	g	2	5	2.63
P	g	1.75		2.39
Ca:P	ratio	1:1	1.6:1	1.10 : 1
K	g	1.1		2.12
Na	g	0.55		0.92
MG	g	0.1		0.26
Cl	g	0.83		0.85
Fe	mg	22	350	25.13
Cu	mg	2.75	7	3.71
Mn	mg	1.4	40	2.69
Zn	mg	25	70	29.56
I	mg	0.38	3	0.47
Se	mg	0.1		0.15

VITAMINS				
	Unit	Min	Max	Recipe
Vit A	IU	1,250		3,717.30
Vit C	mg			41.48
Vit D	IU	125		589.93
Vit E	IU	12.5		12.69
Thiamine, B1	mg	0.45		0.56
Riboflavine, B2	mg	1.05		2.42
Niacin, B3	mg	3.4		24.92
Pantothenic Acid, B5	mg	3		5.48
B6 (Pyridoxine)	mg	0.3		0.98
Vit B12	mg	0.01		0.02
Folic Acid	mg	0.05		0.14
Choline	mg	425		662.13
Vit K1	mg			0.05
Biotin	mg			0.26

FATS				
	Unit	Min	Max	Recipe
Total	g	21.25		51.52
Saturated	g			18.5
Monounsaturated	g			19.42
Polyunsaturated	g			6.93
LA	g	3.25	16.25	3.63
ALA	g	0.2		1.06
AA	g	0.08		0.37
EPA	g			0.51
DPA	g			0.1
DHA	g			0.58
Omega-6/Omega-3	ratio			1.79 : 1
EPA + DHA	g	0.13		1.09

AMINO ACIDS				
	Unit	Min	Max	Recipe
Total protein	g	50		121.83
Tryptophan	g	0.53		1.01
Threonine	g	1.6		4.65
Isoleucine	g	1.25		5.27
Leucine	g	2		9.31
Lysine*	g	1.75	7*	9.62
Methionine	g	0.65		3.43
M - Cystine	g	1.33		4.79
Phenylalanine	g	1.25		4.84
P - Tyrosine	g	2.5		8.81
Valine	g	1.4		5.87
Arginine	g	1.73		8.11
Histidine	g	0.63		3.98
Purines	mg			544.25
Taurine	g			0.19

NB kcal per weight values will vary according to cooking or if raw. The values given are based on cooked as per the recipe.

Masha's Duck

& Almonds

Ducks can be domestic or wild shot, but remove any shot pellets and don't include the bones. If you have no oysters, then replace with 135mg zinc, e.g. 9 capsules at 15mg/cap, and 36mg iron, e.g. 2 capsules at 18mg/cap

Formulated to FEDIAF

Ingredients

593g Duck or chicken gizzard

389g Oysters

185g Beef liver

741g Oily fish

2,965g Duck, 85% lean, no bone

630g Turkey meat, no skin or bone

260g Winter squash

222g Spinach

63g Almonds

93g Turmeric

71g Bonemeal

6g Kelp (I = 700mcg/c)

6g Salt

2,450g Choline, e.g. 7 capsules at 350mg/cap

25g Cod liver oil

Please weigh all ingredients accurately.

You will need a large mixing bowl, tub, or small bucket and a large, sturdy, long-handled spoon to thoroughly mix the recipe.

Method – cooking is optional

1. Finely chop the gizzards, oysters, and liver. Place in the bowl.

2. Twist heads off the fish and add whole.

3. Chop the rest of the fish and all the meat into bite-sized chunks before adding to the mix.

4. Divide the mixture into one or multiple roasting tins, crock pots, or casserole dishes and slow cook in the oven at 212F/100C for 2 to 3 hours until just cooked.

5. Allow to cool, and then use your hands to crumble the mix back into the bowl.

6. Chop and steam the squash until just tender. Add to bowl

7. Chop and steam the spinach to a wilting point, then add to the mix.

8. If you leave the squash and spinach raw, you can juice them both. Add the juice and pulp to the bowl.

9. Chop the almonds before adding

10. Now add all the dry powdered ingredients: turmeric, bonemeal, kelp, & salt

11. Twist open any supplement capsules and sprinkle the powder into the bowl

12. Roughly mix everything until no dry powders are visible

13. Add the cod liver oil, then thoroughly mix the entire recipe

14. Weigh out a suitably sized portion to serve to your puppy.

For the best long-term health, practice body condition scoring, use growth charts, and avoid over- or underfeeding. Refrigerate or freeze the remainder.

See Chapt. 5 for growth charts and portion sizing, Chapt. 6 for substitutions, Chapts. 8-10 for additional method details, tips, & advice, Chapt. 11 for storage info. and Chapt. 12 for online suppliers.

Nutritional Information

MACRONUTRIENT ANALYSIS			
Composition	As formulated	Dry Matter	% kcal
Protein	16.83%	54.57%	42.11%
Fat	9.6%	31.12%	54.05%
Ash	2.25%	7.3%	
Moisture	69.15%		
Fiber	0.63%	2.03%	
Net Carbs	1.54%	4.98%	3.84%
Sugars	0.35%	1.15%	0.88%
Starch	1.13%	3.66%	2.82%
Total			100%

MACRONUTRIENT INFORMATION	
Total kcal in recipe	10,000
kcal / oz	45
kcal / lb	725
kcal / 100g	160
kcal / kg	1,599

MINERALS				
	Unit	Min	Max	Recipe
Ca	g	2	5	2.23
P	g	1.75		2.09
Ca:P	ratio	1:1	1.6:1	1.07:1
K	g	1.1		1.84
Na	g	0.55		0.87
MG	g	0.1		0.22
Cl	g	0.83		0.97
Fe	mg	22	350	22.17
Cu	mg	2.75	7	4.29
Mn	mg	1.4	40	2.62
Zn	mg	25	70	25.38
I	mg	0.38	3	0.46
Se	mg	0.1		0.13

VITAMINS				
	Unit	Min	Max	Recipe
Vit A	IU	1,250		5,052.40
Vit C	mg			10.55
Vit D	IU	125		483.76
Vit E	IU	12.5		12.62
Thiamine, B1	mg	0.45		0.68
Riboflavine, B2	mg	1.05		1.94
Niacin, B3	mg	3.4		35.42
Pantothenic Acid, B5	mg	3		6.7
B6 (Pyridoxine)	mg	0.3		0.8
Vit B12	mg	0.01		0.02
Folic Acid	mg	0.05		0.11
Choline	mg	425		442.44
Vit K1	mg			0.08
Biotin	mg			0.33

FATS				
	Unit	Min	Max	Recipe
Total	g	21.25		60.05
Saturated	g			17.4
Monounsaturated	g			28.94
Polyunsaturated	g			9.15
LA	g	3.25	16.25	6.38
ALA	g	0.2		0.44
AA	g	0.08		0.14
EPA	g			0.66
DPA	g			0.11
DHA	g			0.91
Omega-6/Omega-3	ratio			3.29 : 1
EPA + DHA	g	0.13		1.57

AMINO ACIDS				
	Unit	Min	Max	Recipe
Total protein	g	50		105.28
Tryptophan	g	0.53		1.25
Threonine	g	1.6		4.28
Isoleucine	g	1.25		4.64
Leucine	g	2		8.17
Lysine*	g	1.75	7*	8.55
Methionine	g	0.65		2.78
M - Cystine	g	1.33		4.13
Phenylalanine	g	1.25		4.28
P - Tyrosine	g	2.5		7.92
Valine	g	1.4		5
Arginine	g	1.73		6.62
Histidine	g	0.63		2.7
Purines	mg			987.39
Taurine	g			0.74

NB kcal per weight values will vary according to cooking or if raw. The values given are based on cooked as per the recipe.

Captain Jaq's Fishy Feast
& Oysters

Captain Jaq lives on the coast and loves swimming, kayaking, and paddle boarding with his owners. He is living the adventure of life to the full! If you prefer this recipe to be entirely whole foods, omit the iron supplement and increase turmeric to 175g

Formulated to AAFCO

Ingredients

2,225g Oily fish, e.g. sardines, mackerel etc.

1,821g Ground beef

506g Chicken gizzards

243g Beef liver

319g Oysters

470g Sweet potato

657g Duck necks

405g Egg, whole, no shell

66g Brazil nuts

121g Turmeric

69g Bonemeal

10g Nutritional yeast

9g salt

7g Kelp

36mg Iron, e.g. 1 capsule at 18mg/cap

21g Sunflower oil

24g Cod liver oil

Please weigh all ingredients accurately.

You will need a large mixing bowl, tub, or small bucket and a large, sturdy, long-handled spoon to thoroughly mix the recipe.

Method

1. Pull the heads off the fish and keep them whole, or chop them into chewy treats, bite-sized chunks according to puppy size. Chop the rest of the fish into bite-sized chunks. Add all to the bowl.

2. Grind the gizzards, liver, and oysters to aid even distribution and add to the mix with the ground beef.

3. If you plan to cook, divide the mixture into one or multiple roasting tins, crock pots, or casserole dishes and slow cook in the oven at 212F/100C for 2 to 3 hours until just cooked.

4. Once the fish & meat mix is cooked, allow it to cool, and then use your hands to crumble the mix back into the bowl.

5. Steam the sweet potato and add it to the bowl, or juice it if you prefer to keep things raw. Add both the juice and pulp to the bowl.

6. Grind the duck necks and add them raw to the mix

7. Chop the

8. Grind the

9. Now add all the dry powdered ingredients: spirulina, turmeric, bonemeal, salt & kelp.

10. Twist open any supplement capsules and sprinkle the powder into the bowl

11. Roughly mix everything until no dry powders are visible

12. Add the cod liver oil, then thoroughly mix the entire recipe

13. Weigh out a suitably sized portion to serve to your puppy.

For the best long-term health, practice body condition scoring, use the growth charts, and try not to over- or underfeed. Refrigerate or freeze the remainder.

See Chapt. 5 for growth charts and portion sizing, Chapt. 6 for substitutions, Chapts. 8-10 for additional method details, tips, & advice, Chapt. 11 for storage info. and Chapt. 12 for online suppliers.

Nutritional Information

MACRONUTRIENT ANALYSIS			
Composition	As formulated	Dry Matter	% kcal
Protein	17.11%	56.98%	47.73%
Fat	7.24%	24.1%	45.44%
Ash	2.52%	8.39%	
Moisture	69.96%		
Fiber	0.71%	2.37%	
Net Carbs	2.45%	8.15%	6.83%
Sugars	0.56%	1.87%	1.57%
Starch	1.92%	6.39%	5.35%
Total			100%

MACRONUTRIENT INFORMATION	
Total kcal in recipe	10,000
kcal / oz	41
kcal / lb	651
kcal / 100g	143
kcal / kg	1,434

MINERALS				
	Unit	Min	Max	Recipe
Ca	g	3	4.5	3.1
P	g	2.5	4	2.73
Ca:P	ratio	1:1	2:1	1.14:1
K	g	1.5		2.33
Na	g	0.8		0.91
MG	g	0.15		0.37
Cl	g	1.1		1.17
Fe	mg	22		24.34
Cu	mg	3.1		4.12
Mn	mg	1.8		3.03
Zn	mg	25		27.62
I	mg	0.25	2.75	0.5
Se	mg	0.09		0.29

VITAMINS				
	Unit	Min	Max	Recipe
Vit A	IU	1,250	62,500	9,453.11
Vit C	mg			4.14
Vit D	IU	125	750	745.52
Vit E	IU	12.5		12.75
Thiamine, B1	mg	0.56		0.77
Riboflavine, B2	mg	1.3		2.54
Niacin, B3	mg	3.4		34.74
Pantothenic Acid, B5	mg	3		6.36
B6 (Pyridoxine)	mg	0.38		1.3
Vit B12	mg	0.01		0.03
Folic Acid	mg	0.05		0.14
Choline	mg	340		383.55
Vit K1	mg			0
Biotin	mg			0.45

FATS				
	Unit	Min	Max	Recipe
Total	g	21.3		50.48
Saturated	g			15.32
Monounsaturated	g			19.08
Polyunsaturated	g			8.96
LA	g	3.3		4.13
ALA	g	0.2		0.28
AA	g			0.36
EPA	g			1.25
DPA	g			0.25
DHA	g			2.04
Omega-6/Omega-3	ratio		30:1	1.30 : 1
EPA + DHA	g	0.1		3.29

AMINO ACIDS				
	Unit	Min	Max	Recipe
Total protein	g	56.3		119.34
Tryptophan	g	0.5		1.14
Threonine	g	2.6		4.97
Isoleucine	g	1.78		5.48
Leucine	g	3.23		9.45
Lysine*	g	2.25		9.92
Methionine	g	0.88		3.29
M - Cystine	g	1.75		4.71
Phenylalanine	g	2.08		4.88
P - Tyrosine	g	3.25		8.86
Valine	g	1.7		6.12
Arginine	g	2.5		7.59
Histidine	g	1.1		3.4
Purines	mg			824.62
Taurine	g			0.47

NB kcal per weight values will vary according to cooking or if raw. The values given are based on cooked as per the recipe.

Minnie's Turkey

& Salmon

Turkey is generally readily available and affordable. Gizzards are an excellent source of a wide range of vitamins and minerals, and the necks give us bone. However, poultry bones are best added raw, not cooked, as cooking them can pose a risk, although when pre-ground, this risk is minimal.

Formulated to FEDIAF

Ingredients

3,995g Turkey meat, no skin

649g Turkey gizzards

265g Beef liver

225g Beef kidney

157g Salmon

385g Oysters

999g Turkey necks

320g Edamame beans, prepared

300g Green leafy veg

165g Almonds

120g Sunflower seeds

150g Turmeric

60g Bonemeal

10g Nutritional yeast

9g Kelp (I = 700mcg/g)

350mg Choline e.g. 1 capsule at 350mg/cap

Please weigh all ingredients accurately.

This recipe requires a meat grinder that can cope with poultry bones.

You will need a large mixing bowl, tub, or small bucket and a large, sturdy, long-handled spoon to thoroughly mix the recipe.

Method – cooking is optional. Recommend to keep necks raw.

1. Chop the turkey into bite-sized chunks and add to bowl

2. Grind the gizzards, liver, kidney, oysters, and salmon, then add to the bowl

3. Divide the mixture into 1 or multiple roasting tins, crock pots, or casserole dishes and slow cook in the oven at 212F/100C for around 3 to 4 hours until cooked.

4. Once the meat mix is cooked, allow it to cool, and then crumble it back into the bowl with your hands.

5. Grind the turkey necks and add to the mix raw

6. Add the edamame beans

7. Chop and lightly steam the leafy veg before adding

8. Chop the almonds and add to the bowl

9. Grind the sunflower seeds before adding to the mix

10. Now add all the dry powdered ingredients: turmeric, bonemeal, yeast, & kelp

11. Twist open any supplement capsules and sprinkle the powder into the bowl

12. Thoroughly mix the entire recipe

13. Weigh out a suitably sized portion to serve to your puppy.

For the best long-term health, practice body condition scoring, use the growth charts, and try not to over- or underfeed. Refrigerate or freeze the remainder.

See Chapt. 5 for growth charts and portion sizing, Chapt. 6 for substitutions, Chapts. 8-10 for additional method details, tips, & advice, Chapt. 11 for storage info. and Chapt. 12 for online suppliers.

Nutritional Information

MACRONUTRIENT ANALYSIS			
Composition	As formulated	Dry Matter	% kcal
Protein	18.34%	63.79%	57.35%
Fat	5.46%	18.99%	38.41%
Ash	2.39%	8.31%	
Moisture	71.25%		
Fiber	1.21%	4.19%	
Net Carbs	1.36%	4.72%	4.24%
Sugars	0.47%	1.63%	1.46%
Starch	1.35%	4.7%	4.23%
Total			100%

MACRONUTRIENT INFORMATION			
Total kcal in recipe			10,000
kcal / oz			36
kcal / lb			580
kcal / 100g			128
kcal / kg			1,279

MINERALS				
	Unit	Min	Max	Recipe
Ca	g	2	5	3.16
P	g	1.75		2.82
Ca:P	ratio	1:1	1.6:1	1.12 : 1
K	g	1.1		2.34
Na	g	0.55		1.21
MG	g	0.1		0.46
Cl	g	0.83		1.19
Fe	mg	22	350	22.55
Cu	mg	2.75	7	5.09
Mn	mg	1.4	40	4.59
Zn	mg	25	70	34.16
I	mg	0.38	3	0.66
Se	mg	0.1		0.19

VITAMINS				
	Unit	Min	Max	Recipe
Vit A	IU	1,250		5,342.02
Vit C	mg			12.36
Vit D	IU	125		125.13
Vit E	IU	12.5		13.79
Thiamine, B1	mg	0.45		0.91
Riboflavine, B2	mg	1.05		3.49
Niacin, B3	mg	3.4		37.75
Pantothenic Acid, B5	mg	3		7.65
B6 (Pyridoxine)	mg	0.3		1.72
Vit B12	mg	0.01		0.03
Folic Acid	mg	0.05		0.25
Choline	mg	425		425.89
Vit K1	mg			0.11
Biotin	mg			0.38

FATS				
	Unit	Min	Max	Recipe
Total	g	21.25		42.68
Saturated	g			8.91
Monounsaturated	g			15.5
Polyunsaturated	g			12.47
LA	g	3.25	16.25	10.24
ALA	g	0.2		0.47
AA	g	0.08		0.37
EPA	g			0.23
DPA	g			0.06
DHA	g			0.23
Omega-6/Omega-3	ratio			10.95 : 1
EPA + DHA	g	0.13		0.47

AMINO ACIDS				
	Unit	Min	Max	Recipe
Total protein	g	50		143.37
Tryptophan	g	0.53		1.57
Threonine	g	1.6		5.3
Isoleucine	g	1.25		4.66
Leucine	g	2		10.26
Lysine*	g	1.75	7*	11.31
Methionine	g	0.65		3.63
M - Cystine	g	1.33		5.14
Phenylalanine	g	1.25		5.13
P - Tyrosine	g	2.5		9.57
Valine	g	1.4		5.26
Arginine	g	1.73		8.75
Histidine	g	0.63		3.86
Purines	mg			1,062.30
Taurine	g			1.33

NB kcal per weight values will vary according to cooking or if raw. The values given are based on cooked as per the recipe.

Georgio's Pork

& Mushrooms

Georgio was exported to Kenya as the first NUA/LUA Dally and lives in a wonderful home there. His show name is Gwydion. My husband was born in Kenya, and our eldest son's name is Gwydion. So it felt like a complete circle to send a Gwydion home to Kenya!

Formulated to FEDIAF

Ingredients

1,910g Pork, lean

1,910g Chicken, mixed meat, no skin or bone, 85% lean

202g Beef liver

141g Beef spleen

655g Oysters

305g Duck egg, whole, no shell. It can be substituted for hen's eggs if necessary.

153g Brown rice, cooked

153g Brown or Italian or crimini mushrooms

67g Hempseed

92g Turmeric

84g Bonemeal

50g Spirulina

8g Nutritional yeast

7g Salt

7g Kelp

1,400mg Choline, e.g. 4 capsules at 350mg/cap

35g Cod liver oil

Please weigh all ingredients accurately.

You will need a large mixing bowl, tub or small bucket and a large, sturdy, long-handled spoon to thoroughly mix the recipe.

Method – please cook the Pork. The rest of the cooking is optional

1. Wrap the pork well and slow cook in the oven at 212F/100C for 3 to 4 hours until cooked and the juices run clear. If you also want to cook the chicken, liver, spleen, and oysters, add them all to the slow roast.

2. Shred the cooked meat into your mixing bowl

3. If you have not cooked the other meats, grind and add them now.

4. Add the eggs and rice.

5. Chop and lightly saute the mushrooms before adding

6. Grind the hempseed and add to the mix

7. Now add all the dry powdered ingredients: turmeric, bonemeal, spirulina, yeast, salt & kelp.

8. Twist open any supplement capsules and sprinkle the powder into the bowl

9. Roughly mix everything until no dry powders are visible

10. Add the cod liver oil, then thoroughly mix the entire recipe

11. Weigh out a suitably sized portion to serve to your puppy.

For the best long-term health, practice body condition scoring, use the growth charts, and try not to over- or underfeed. Refrigerate or freeze the remainder.

See Chapt. 5 for growth charts and portion sizing, Chapt. 6 for substitutions, Chapts. 8-10 for additional method details, tips, & advice, Chapt. 11 for storage info. and Chapt. 12 for online suppliers.

Nutritional Information

MACRONUTRIENT ANALYSIS			
Composition	As formulated	Dry Matter	% kcal
Protein	21.18%	57.76%	46.65%
Fat	9.74%	26.55%	48.25%
Ash	2.82%	7.69%	
Moisture	63.33%		
Fiber	0.62%	1.7%	
Net Carbs	2.31%	6.31%	5.09%
Sugars	0.36%	0.98%	0.79%
Starch	1.79%	4.89%	3.95%
Total			100%

MACRONUTRIENT INFORMATION					
Total kcal in recipe					10,000
kcal / oz					52
kcal / lb					823
kcal / 100g					182
kcal / kg					1,816

MINERALS				
	Unit	Min	Max	Recipe
Ca	g	2	5	2.6
P	g	1.75		2.49
Ca:P	ratio	1:1	1.6:1	1.04 : 1
K	g	1.1		2.11
Na	g	0.55		0.83
MG	g	0.1		0.26
Cl	g	0.83		1.03
Fe	mg	22	350	23.56
Cu	mg	2.75	7	3.85
Mn	mg	1.4	40	3.2
Zn	mg	25	70	25.02
I	mg	0.38	3	0.46
Se	mg	0.1		0.18

VITAMINS				
	Unit	Min	Max	Recipe
Vit A	IU	1,250		3,439.41
Vit C	mg			8.46
Vit D	IU	125		482.97
Vit E	IU	12.5		12.53
Thiamine, B1	mg	0.45		1.49
Riboflavine, B2	mg	1.05		2.63
Niacin, B3	mg	3.4		35.03
Pantothenic Acid, B5	mg	3		6.19
B6 (Pyridoxine)	mg	0.3		1.5
Vit B12	mg	0.01		0.02
Folic Acid	mg	0.05		0.11
Choline	mg	425		425.26
Vit K1	mg			0
Biotin	mg			0.34

FATS				
	Unit	Min	Max	Recipe
Total	g	21.25		53.62
Saturated	g			14.23
Monounsaturated	g			19.4
Polyunsaturated	g			13.3
LA	g	3.25	16.25	9.04
ALA	g	0.2		1.22
AA	g	0.08		0.74
EPA	g			0.45
DPA	g			0.12
DHA	g			0.54
Omega-6/Omega-3	ratio			4.23 : 1
EPA + DHA	g	0.13		1

AMINO ACIDS				
	Unit	Min	Max	Recipe
Total protein	g	50		116.63
Tryptophan	g	0.53		1.43
Threonine	g	1.6		5.01
Isoleucine	g	1.25		5.45
Leucine	g	2		9.33
Lysine*	g	1.75	7*	9.66
Methionine	g	0.65		3.14
M - Cystine	g	1.33		4.65
Phenylalanine	g	1.25		4.96
P - Tyrosine	g	2.5		9.48
Valine	g	1.4		5.99
Arginine	g	1.73		7.82
Histidine	g	0.63		3.97
Purines	mg			712.49
Taurine	g			0.41

NB kcal per weight values will vary according to cooking or if raw. The values given are based on cooked as per the recipe.

80% adult weight to maturity

Low purine

These are balanced and low-purine recipes. They include a range of raw and cooked recipes. By necessity, these contain more supplementation, as the necessary nutrient balance for puppies cannot readily be achieved solely through whole foods with no organ meat, oily fish, oysters, or other high-purine ingredients.

You can always 'step back' and feed recipes for the previous age group, just don't jump forwards to an older age group recipe.

Low purine recipes can be fed to any other puppies but dogs with hyperuricosuria must only be fed from the low purine recipe range.

Pebble's Cheesy Pork

& Rabbit

Pork is a great low-purine protein source and is sadly overlooked due to concerns over its safety for dogs. However, provided it is cooked, there is no problem at all. The concern centers around a potential parasite that can occasionally be found in raw pork, so yes, cook it, but don't miss out on the opportunity to provide this additional variety for dogs with hyperuricosuria.

Formulated to FEDIAF. Balanced COOKED or RAW with just the Pork COOKED

Ingredients

2,183g Pork, no visible fat

1,572g Beef tripe

1,163g Rabbit meat only, no visible fat

873g Full-fat cottage cheese

291g Egg, whole, no shell

630g Cabbage

391g Sunflower or Safflower seeds

131g Turmeric powder

117g Bonemeal

9g Salt

7g Kelp powder

120mg Zinc, typically 8 capsules at 15mg/cap

18mg Copper, typically 9 capsules at 2mg/cap

25g Cod liver oil

Please weigh all ingredients accurately.

You will need a large mixing bowl, tub, or small bucket and a large, sturdy, long-handled spoon to thoroughly mix the recipe.

Method – we recommend cooking the pork at least

1. Wrap the pork well and slowly cook in the oven at 212F/100C for around 3 to 4 hours until the juices are cooked. Add it to the slow roast if you also want to cook the tripe or rabbit.

2. Shred the cooked meat into your mixing bowl

3. If you have not cooked the tripe, add it raw and ground.

4. If you have not cooked the rabbit, cut it into bite-sized chunks and add it raw to the bowl now.

5. Add the cottage cheese and eggs

6. Chop the cabbage and steam it if desired before adding it to the mix

7. Grind the sunflower seeds before adding them as well

8. Now add all the dry powdered ingredients: turmeric, bonemeal, salt & kelp

9. Twist open supplement capsules and sprinkle the powder into the bowl

10. Roughly mix everything until no dry powders are visible

11. Add the cod liver oil, then thoroughly mix the entire recipe

12. Weigh out a suitably sized portion to serve to your puppy.

For the best long-term health, practice body condition scoring, use the growth charts, and try not to over- or underfeed. Refrigerate or freeze the remainder.

See Chapt. 5 for growth charts and portion sizing, Chapt. 6 for substitutions, Chapts. 8-10 for additional method details, tips, & advice, Chapt. 11 for storage info. and Chapt. 12 for online suppliers.

Nutritional Information

MACRONUTRIENT ANALYSIS			
Composition	As formulated	Dry Matter	% kcal
Protein	22.5%	58.97%	50.17%
Fat	7.89%	20.68%	42.72%
Ash	3.35%	8.77%	
Moisture	61.84%		
Fiber	1.23%	3.22%	
Net Carbs	3.19%	8.37%	7.12%
Sugars	0.89%	2.33%	1.98%
Starch	1.62%	4.25%	3.61%
Total			100%

MACRONUTRIENT INFORMATION				
Total kcal in recipe				10,000
kcal / oz				45
kcal / lb				712
kcal / 100g				157
kcal / kg				1,570

MINERALS				
	Unit	Min	Max	Recipe
Ca	g	2	5	4.02
P	g	1.75		3.59
Ca:P	ratio	1:1	1.6:1	1.12 : 1
K	g	1.1		2.7
Na	g	0.55		1.11
MG	g	0.1		0.4
Cl	g	0.83		0.84
Fe	mg	22	350	22.01
Cu	mg	2.75	7	2.97
Mn	mg	1.4	40	4.73
Zn	mg	25	70	26.16
I	mg	0.38	3	0.41
Se	mg	0.1		0.17

VITAMINS				
	Unit	Min	Max	Recipe
Vit A	IU	1,250		1,266.82
Vit C	mg			20.47
Vit D	IU	125		308.02
Vit E	IU	12.5		32.54
Thiamine, B1	mg	0.45		0.96
Riboflavine, B2	mg	1.05		1.34
Niacin, B3	mg	3.4		28.8
Pantothenic Acid, B5	mg	3		3.31
B6 (Pyridoxine)	mg	0.3		1.08
Vit B12	mg	0.01		0.01
Folic Acid	mg	0.05		0.09
Choline	mg	425		439
Vit K1	mg			0.03
Biotin	mg			0.07

FATS				
	Unit	Min	Max	Recipe
Total	g	21.25		50.26
Saturated	g			14.16
Monounsaturated	g			17.95
Polyunsaturated	g			12.26
LA	g	3.25	16.25	10.36
ALA	g	0.2		0.41
AA	g	0.08		0.25
EPA	g			0.17
DPA	g			0.04
DHA	g			0.21
Omega-6/Omega-3	ratio			11.66 : 1
EPA + DHA	g	0.13		0.38

AMINO ACIDS				
	Unit	Min	Max	Recipe
Total protein	g	50		143.33
Tryptophan	g	0.53		1.82
Threonine	g	1.6		5.98
Isoleucine	g	1.25		6.57
Leucine	g	2		11.44
Lysine*	g	1.75	7*	11.73
Methionine	g	0.65		3.8
M - Cystine	g	1.33		5.49
Phenylalanine	g	1.25		6.16
P - Tyrosine	g	2.5		11.71
Valine	g	1.4		7.51
Arginine	g	1.73		9.7
Histidine	g	0.63		4.91
Purines	mg			454.23
Taurine	g			0.11

NB kcal per weight values will vary according to cooking or if raw. The values given are based on cooked as per the recipe.

Dom's Fish

& Broccoli

Dom is an absolutely stunning Spanish champion stud dog and our first AI sire. The process was hugely successful and resulted in a beautiful litter of 10 strong, healthy puppies, several of whom entered the show ring themselves.

Formulated to FEDIAF. Balanced COOKED or RAW

Ingredients

2,263g Whitefish

1,679g Chicken breast, no skin

1,132g Rabbit, lean, no skin

962g Chicken heart

849g Chicken gizzard

679g Egg, whole, no shell

350g Broccoli

300g Carrots

187g Turmeric

96g Bonemeal

10g Kelp (I = 700mcg/g)

6g Salt

180mg Zinc, e.g. 12 capsules at 15mg/cap

16mg Copper, e.g. 8 capsules at 2mg/cap

12g Cod liver oil

Please weigh all ingredients accurately.

You will need a large mixing bowl, tub, or small bucket and a large, sturdy, long-handled spoon to thoroughly mix the recipe.

Method – cooking is optional

1. Chop or grind all the meats so that roughly half is in bite-sized chunks and the remainder is ground.

2. Mix the meats together and add the egg.

3. If cooking, divide the mixture into one or more roasting tins, crock pots, or casserole dishes and slow cook in the oven at 212F/100C for 2 to 3 hours until cooked.

4. If cooking, steam the broccoli & carrots until just tender.

5. If raw, juice the carrots and broccoli and add both juice and pulp to the mixing bowl. If you don't have a juicer, chop the florets and grate the stems and carrots.

6. Once the meat and fish mix is cooked, allow it to cool, and then use your hands to crumble the mix back into the bowl.

7. Now add all the dry powdered ingredients: spirulina, turmeric, bonemeal, kelp & salt.

8. Twist open any supplement capsules and sprinkle the powder into the bowl

9. Roughly mix everything until no dry powders are visible

10. Add the cod liver oil, then thoroughly mix the entire recipe

11. Weigh out a suitably sized portion to serve to your puppy.

For the best long-term health, practice body condition scoring, use the growth charts, and try not to over- or underfeed. Refrigerate or freeze the remainder.

See Chapt. 5 for growth charts and portion sizing, Chapt. 6 for substitutions, Chapts. 8-10 for additional method details, tips, & advice, Chapt. 11 for storage info. and Chapt. 12 for online suppliers.

Nutritional Information

MACRONUTRIENT ANALYSIS			
Composition	As formulated	Dry Matter	% kcal
Protein	17.81%	68.08%	63.76%
Fat	3.83%	14.64%	30.86%
Ash	2.29%	8.75%	
Moisture	73.84%		
Fiber	0.73%	2.79%	
Net Carbs	1.5%	5.74%	5.38%
Sugars	0.44%	1.67%	1.56%
Starch	1.18%	4.5%	4.21%
Total			100%

MACRONUTRIENT INFORMATION				
Total kcal in recipe				10,000
kcal / oz				32
kcal / lb				507
kcal / 100g				112
kcal / kg				1,117

MINERALS				
	Unit	Min	Max	Recipe
Ca	g	2	5	3.15
P	g	1.75		3.08
Ca:P	ratio	1:1	1.6:1	1.02 : 1
K	g	1.1		2.91
Na	g	0.55		0.97
MG	g	0.1		0.28
Cl	g	0.83		1.2
Fe	mg	22	350	26.83
Cu	mg	2.75	7	2.83
Mn	mg	1.4	40	4.32
Zn	mg	25	70	29.04
I	mg	0.38	3	0.79
Se	mg	0.1		0.21

VITAMINS				
	Unit	Min	Max	Recipe
Vit A	IU	1,250		5,762.04
Vit C	mg			45.13
Vit D	IU	125		597.11
Vit E	IU	12.5		13.95
Thiamine, B1	mg	0.45		0.69
Riboflavine, B2	mg	1.05		1.89
Niacin, B3	mg	3.4		44.91
Pantothenic Acid, B5	mg	3		8.82
B6 (Pyridoxine)	mg	0.3		3.04
Vit B12	mg	0.01		0.03
Folic Acid	mg	0.05		0.24
Choline	mg	425		776.8
Vit K1	mg			0.05
Biotin	mg			0.31

FATS				
	Unit	Min	Max	Recipe
Total	g	21.25		34.29
Saturated	g			9.35
Monounsaturated	g			9.98
Polyunsaturated	g			7.92
LA	g	3.25	16.25	4.51
ALA	g	0.2		0.45
AA	g	0.08		1.16
EPA	g			0.38
DPA	g			0.04
DHA	g			0.84
Omega-6/Omega-3	ratio			3.38 : 1
EPA + DHA	g	0.13		1.21

AMINO ACIDS				
	Unit	Min	Max	Recipe
Total protein	g	50		159.41
Tryptophan	g	0.53		1.9
Threonine	g	1.6		7.02
Isoleucine	g	1.25		7.81
Leucine	g	2		12.54
Lysine*	g	1.75	7*	13.48
Methionine	g	0.65		4.27
M - Cystine	g	1.33		6.29
Phenylalanine	g	1.25		6.6
P - Tyrosine	g	2.5		12.09
Valine	g	1.4		8.24
Arginine	g	1.73		10.03
Histidine	g	0.63		4.39
Purines	mg			1,026.15
Taurine	g			0.47

NB kcal per weight values will vary according to cooking or if raw. The values given are based on cooked as per the recipe.

Bonus Adult Recipe

Ina with a bundle of pups

We are in the process of writing an adult fresh-feeding recipe book but here is a freebie to get you started.

Sign up for our mailing list on ridgehilldogs.com if you would like a free advance copy of upcoming book releases, including our dog treat book and healthy, balanced homemade adult dog recipes.

Ina's Delux Mix

With Everything!

Ina is our first Normal Uric acid-breeding Dalmatian. She has been an outstanding mother, raising 29 beautiful puppies and proving to be the best grandma possible by helping her daughter – even coming in milk to help feed and care for her grandchildren!

The problem with this recipe mix is not the wide meat variety, that's just a case of having an organized freezer, no, no, it's the slippery kitchen floor. As the girls watch our every move, they drool excessively!

Other great things about this recipe that make the effort worthwhile: It is so nutritionally rich due to the wide range of meats and offal. The specification for adult dogs is also less demanding regarding precise balance. As a result, you can add mixed vegetables without unbalancing any of the minerals, vitamins, and fats. We use this recipe as a base and add vegetables to bulk their meals in a low-calorie way if our girls are getting a little plump. They get the same great flavors and balanced nutrition but fewer calories. This recipe can cope with being bulked up to double in weight with mixed vegetables without going out of balance or requiring any supplementation.

Formulated to FEDIAF. Balanced RAW.

Ingredients

862g Beef tripe
862g Oily fish
862g Ground lamb 85% lean
862g Ground Beef 80% lean
862g Turkey necks
431g Chicken gizzards
302g Oysters
216g Salmon
216g Chicken feet
216g Beef spleen
216g Beef heart
216g Beef kidney

56g Bonemeal

48g Turmeric

10g Nutritional yeast

9g Kelp

14g Cod liver oil

Please weigh all ingredients accurately.

This recipe requires a meat grinder that can cope with poultry bones.

You will need a large mixing bowl, tub, or small bucket and a large, sturdy, long-handled spoon to thoroughly mix the recipe.

Method

1. Look at all your meat and fish. It likely comes in various forms. You ideally want approximately half of the mix to end up ground and half chopped into bite-sized chunks, so decide what to chop up and what to grind to achieve this. Leave fish heads whole when possible, as they lend a chewy, crunchy texture to the mix.

2. Put all that meat and fish into your bowl and mix roughly

3. Add all the dry ingredients

4. Mix thoroughly

5. If you plan to add vegetables, you can now add them chopped, or you can store the recipe like it is and add vegetables each day according to what you have and how your dog's condition is looking.

Practice body condition scoring and try not to over or under-feed for the best long-term health.

Refrigerate or freeze the remainder.

See Chapt. 5 for growth charts and portion sizing, Chapt. 6 for substitutions, Chapts. 8-10 for additional method details, tips, & advice, Chapt. 11 for storage info. and Chapt. 12 for online suppliers.

Nutritional Information

MACRONUTRIENT ANALYSIS			
Composition	As formulated	Dry Matter	% kcal
Protein	17.22%	57.86%	44.59%
Fat	9.05%	30.39%	52.7%
Ash	2.23%	7.5%	
Moisture	70.24%		
Fiber	0.22%	0.73%	
Net Carbs	1.04%	3.51%	2.71%
Sugars	0.21%	0.71%	0.55%
Starch	0.64%	2.15%	1.66%
Total			100%

MACRONUTRIENT INFORMATION	
Total kcal in recipe	10,000
kcal / oz	44
kcal / lb	701
kcal / 100g	155
kcal / kg	1,545

MINERALS				
	Unit	Min	Max	Recipe
Ca	g	1.25	6.25	2.84
P	g	1	4	2.35
Ca:P	ratio	1:1	02:01	1.21 : 1
K	g	1.25		1.73
Na	g	0.25		0.59
MG	g	0.18		0.28
Cl	g	0.38		0.52
Fe	mg	9	170	25.37
Cu	mg	1.8	7	3.67
Mn	mg	1.44	42.5	1.49
Zn	mg	18	56.8	26.52
I	mg	0.26	2.75	0.67
Se	mg	0.08		0.17

VITAMINS				
	Unit	Min	Max	Recipe
Vit A	IU	1,515	100,000	4,339.75
Vit C	mg			15.56
Vit D	IU	138	568	517.8
Vit E	IU	9		10.07
Thiamine, B1	mg	0.54		1.27
Riboflavine, B2	mg	1.5		2.9
Niacin, B3	mg	4.09		34.35
Pantothenic Acid, B5	mg	3.55		6.31
B6 (Pyridoxine)	mg	0.36		2.1
Vit B12	mg	0.01		0.04
Folic Acid	mg	0.07		0.2
Choline	mg	409		587.02
Vit K1	mg			0.01
Biotin	mg			0.34

FATS				
	Unit	Min	Max	Recipe
Total	g	13.75		58.56
Saturated	g			20.66
Monounsaturated	g			21.83
Polyunsaturated	g			7.5
LA	g	3.27		4.16
ALA	g			0.46
AA	g			0.38
EPA	g			0.71
DPA	g			0.18
DHA	g			1.05
Omega-6/Omega-3	ratio			2.06 : 1
EPA + DHA	g			1.76

AMINO ACIDS				
	Unit	Min	Max	Recipe
Total protein	g	45		111.48
Tryptophan	g	0.43		1.09
Threonine	g	1.3		4.43
Isoleucine	g	1.15		4.69
Leucine	g	2.05		8.36
Lysine*	g	1.05		8.99
Methionine	g	1		2.98
M - Cystine	g	1.91		4.24
Phenylalanine	g	1.35		4.29
P - Tyrosine	g	2.23		7.88
Valine	g	1.48		5.18
Arginine	g	1.3		6.81
Histidine	g	0.58		3.22
Purines	mg			650.89
Taurine	g			0.4

*NB kcal per weight values will vary according to cooking or if raw. The following values are based on lightly cooked.

Bonus Training Treat Recipes

For Puppies of all ages like Holly & Magick here

Don't worry. We are also writing a treat recipe book. Can we fully balance treats so we don't have to worry about how many we use for training? Well, yes – and no! Keep an eye on your puppy or dog's all-important waistline with Body Condition Scoring (Chapter 5—remember?). Treats fit a lot of calories into a small space to be highly rewarding and appealing for training. So yes, they are fully balanced, but they are not really an appropriate meal recipe substitute. There are two Recipes here: one standard recipe, Gwyniera's Training Treats, and one low in purines for our Dallies. As always, the low-purine recipe is suitable for all dogs. Both are fully balanced and suitable for puppies from weaning onwards.

Sign up for our mailing list on ridgehilldogs.com if you want a free advance copy of upcoming books released, including our dog treat book and healthy, balanced, homemade adult dog recipes. Please don't forget to share your view of this book on Amazon so that other puppy owners can benefit from it. As independent publishers, it makes all the difference to us when you leave a review, and we read each and every one of them. Thank you.

Gwyniera's Training Treats

Tempting & Delicious

Gwyniera, also known as Baby, loves to be cuddled and hugged at any time of the day. She is nearly 4 now and still enjoys weekly group training, performing in obedience and agility classes. These treats are some of her favorites, but they don't necessarily stop her from turning to the right when I'm fairly certain I called out left!

Formulated to FEDIAF. This recipe makes 2,200kcals worth of treats. Balanced COOKED

Ingredients

481g Oily fish

224g Oysters

319g Beef heart

54g Beef liver

260g Black beans, canned, no need to rinse

317g Eggs, whole, no shell

20g Bonemeal

10g Turmeric

8g Kelp

4g Cod liver oil

3g Sunflower oil

Please weigh all ingredients accurately.

This recipe requires a blender. Baking mats suitable for dog treats are preferable, but these can be baked on a lined baking tray.

Method

1. The whole fish is placed into a blender with the oysters, heart, and liver. Add water as necessary and blend to a thick batter.

2. Add the can of beans and the eggs. Whizz briefly.

3. Add all the dry ingredients and oil. Blend until smooth, adding water if needed to create a thick batter.

4. Now you have a choice. 1: Pour the mixture into silicon baking mats with small indentations suitable for dog treats or, 2: Pour the mixture into a baking tin lined with greaseproof paper

5. Bake very slowly in a low oven at 212F / 100C for about an hour or until the treats are shrinking from the sides.

6. Remove from the oven. If you have baking mats then allow to cool completely before popping the treats out. If in a big flat tray then cut the treats with a sharp knife or pizza wheel as they are still cooling then leave in the tray until cold. Smaller is better for training treats.

7. Store in the fridge for up to a week or freezer up to 3 months. You can use them straight from the freezer, no need to defrost.

See Chapt. 5 for growth charts and portion sizing, Chapt. 6 for substitutions, Chapts. 8-10 for additional method details, tips, & advice, Chapt. 11 for storage info. and Chapt. 12 for online suppliers.

Nutritional Information

MACRONUTRIENT ANALYSIS			
Composition	As formulated	Dry Matter	% kcal
Protein	18.1%	55.69%	50.37%
Fat	6.34%	19.51%	39.7%
Ash	2.96%	9.11%	
Moisture	67.5%		
Fiber	1.53%	4.7%	
Net Carbs	3.57%	10.98%	9.93%
Sugars	0.49%	1.49%	1.35%
Starch	1.27%	3.91%	3.54%
Total			100%

MACRONUTRIENT INFORMATION	
Total kcal in recipe	2,000
kcal / oz	41
kcal / lb	652
kcal / 100g	144
kcal / kg	1,437

MINERALS				
	Unit	Min	Max	Recipe
Ca	g	1.25	6.25	3.27
P	g	1	4	2.94
Ca:P	ratio	1:1	02:01	1.11 : 1
K	g	1.25		2.45
Na	g	0.25		1.18
MG	g	0.18		0.31
Cl	g	0.38		1.16
Fe	mg	9	170	26.47
Cu	mg	1.8	7	6.96
Mn	mg	1.44	42.5	2.28
Zn	mg	18	56.8	49.16
I	mg	0.26	2.75	2.75
Se	mg	0.08		0.22

VITAMINS				
	Unit	Min	Max	Recipe
Vit A	IU	1,515	100,000	4,115.60
Vit C	mg			8.65
Vit D	IU	138	568	746.68
Vit E	IU	9		15.04
Thiamine, B1	mg	0.54		0.55
Riboflavine, B2	mg	1.5		3.3
Niacin, B3	mg	4.09		30.73
Pantothenic Acid, B5	mg	3.55		6.55
B6 (Pyridoxine)	mg	0.36		0.74
Vit B12	mg	0.01		0.04
Folic Acid	mg	0.07		0.24
Choline	mg	409		641.12
Vit K1	mg			0
Biotin	mg			0.49

FATS				
	Unit	Min	Max	Recipe
Total	g	13.75		44.11
Saturated	g			12.08
Monounsaturated	g			15.64
Polyunsaturated	g			9.59
LA	g	3.27		3.6
ALA	g			0.37
AA	g			0.61
EPA	g			1.25
DPA	g			0.23
DHA	g			1.9
Omega-6/Omega-3	ratio			1.01 : 1
EPA + DHA	g			3.16

AMINO ACIDS				
	Unit	Min	Max	Recipe
Total protein	g	45		125.92
Tryptophan	g	0.43		1.45
Threonine	g	1.3		5.02
Isoleucine	g	1.15		5.78
Leucine	g	2.05		10.08
Lysine*	g	1.05		10.29
Methionine	g	1		3.59
M - Cystine	g	1.91		5.12
Phenylalanine	g	1.35		5.41
P - Tyrosine	g	2.23		9.75
Valine	g	1.48		6.63
Arginine	g	1.3		7.91
Histidine	g	0.58		3.65
Purines	mg			989.29
Taurine	g			0.48

*NB kcal per weight values will vary according to cooking or if raw. The following values are based on lightly cooked.

Low Purine Training treats

With Peanuts & Parmesan

This recipe makes 2,200 kcal worth of treats—bear this in mind when using. You can weigh them into batches of a set number of kcals to maintain awareness of how much you are feeding. For example, little bags of 100, 300, or 500 kcals according to the size of your puppy and whether you are thinking in terms of a day or a week's allowance.

Formulated to FEDIAF. Balanced COOKED

Ingredients

40g Chia seeds

130g Sweet potato

81g Peanuts, no salt

8g Brazil nuts

110g Chicken gizzards

110g Beef heart

110g Chicken heart

85g Beef tripe

110g Parmesan cheese

215g Egg, whole, no shell

22g Bonemeal

6g Kelp

2g salt

700mg Choline, e.g. 2 capsules at 350mg/cap

45mg Zing, e.g. 3 capsules at 15mg/cap

36mg Iron, e.g. 2 capsules at 18mg/cap

4mg Copper, e.g. 2 capsules at 2mg/cap

16g Cod liver oil

Please weigh all ingredients accurately.

This recipe requires a blender. Baking mats suitable for dog treats are preferable but these can be baked in a lined baking tray.

Method

1. Grind the chia seeds and soak them in about an inch of water. They will become gloopy, which helps bind the recipe.

2. Steam the sweet potato until soft

3. Chop the peanuts and Brazil nuts until they start to become butter

4. Put the gizzards, hearts, and tripe in a blender and add sufficient water to blend into a thick batter

5. Finely grate the parmesan and add to the blender

6. Add the eggs and give the blender a quick whizz

7. Now add everything else: the chia seeds, sweet potato, dry ingredients, supplements (empty the capsules), and oil

8. Blend until smooth, adding water if required to create a thick batter

9. Now you have a choice. 1: Pour the mixture into silicon baking mats with small indentations suitable for dog treats or 2: Pour the mixture into a baking tin lined with greaseproof paper

10. Bake slowly in a low oven at 212F / 100C for about an hour or until the treats shrink from the sides.

11. Remove from the oven. If you have baking mats, allow them to cool completely before popping the treats out. If they are in a big flat tray, cut the treats with a sharp knife or pizza wheel while they are still cooling, and leave them in the tray until cold. Smaller is better for training treats.

12. Store in the fridge for up to a week or freezer for up to 3 months. You can use them straight from the freezer; there is no need to defrost.

See Chapt. 5 for growth charts and portion sizing, Chapt. 6 for substitutions, Chapts. 8-10 for additional method details, tips, & advice, Chapt. 11 for storage info. and Chapt. 12 for online suppliers.

Nutritional Information

MACRONUTRIENT ANALYSIS

Composition	As formulated	Dry Matter	% kcal
Protein	17.45%	36.84%	28.94%
Fat	16.15%	34.09%	60.27%
Ash	4.72%	9.97%	
Moisture	52.64%		
Fiber	2.54%	5.37%	
Net Carbs	6.5%	13.73%	10.79%
Sugars	1.39%	2.94%	2.31%
Starch	2.21%	4.66%	3.66%
Total			100%

MACRONUTRIENT INFORMATION

Total kcal in recipe	2,200
kcal / oz	68
kcal / lb	1,093
kcal / 100g	241
kcal / kg	2,411

MINERALS

	Unit	Min	Max	Recipe
Ca	g	1.25	6.25	3.57
P	g	1	4	2.44
Ca:P	ratio	1:1	02:01	1.46 : 1
K	g	1.25		1.32
Na	g	0.25		1.68
MG	g	0.18		0.27
Cl	g	0.38		0.87
Fe	mg	9	170	28.98
Cu	mg	1.8	7	3.17
Mn	mg	1.44	42.5	1.61
Zn	mg	18	56.8	29.87
I	mg	0.26	2.75	1.77
Se	mg	0.08		0.16

VITAMINS				
	Unit	Min	Max	Recipe
Vit A	IU	1,515	100,000	7,263.76
Vit C	mg			4.14
Vit D	IU	138	568	911.16
Vit E	IU	9		31.68
Thiamine, B1	mg	0.54		0.45
Riboflavine, B2	mg	1.5		1.45
Niacin, B3	mg	4.09		11.32
Pantothenic Acid, B5	mg	3.55		3.64
B6 (Pyridoxine)	mg	0.36		0.33
Vit B12	mg	0.01		0.01
Folic Acid	mg	0.07		0.18
Choline	mg	409		537.85
Vit K1	mg			0
Biotin	mg			0.12

FATS				
	Unit	Min	Max	Recipe
Total	g	13.75		66.96
Saturated	g			18.38
Monounsaturated	g			24.36
Polyunsaturated	g			17.19
LA	g	3.27		10.05
ALA	g			3.71
AA	g			0.64
EPA	g			0.5
DPA	g			0.07
DHA	g			0.61
Omega-6/Omega-3	ratio			1.95 : 1
EPA + DHA	g			1.11

AMINO ACIDS				
	Unit	Min	Max	Recipe
Total protein	g	45		72.36
Tryptophan	g	0.43		0.85
Threonine	g	1.3		2.9
Isoleucine	g	1.15		3.37
Leucine	g	2.05		5.76
Lysine*	g	1.05		4.96
Methionine	g	1		1.88
M - Cystine	g	1.91		2.76
Phenylalanine	g	1.35		3.46
P - Tyrosine	g	2.23		6.35
Valine	g	1.48		3.92
Arginine	g	1.3		5.07
Histidine	g	0.58		1.96
Purines	mg			253.2
Taurine	g			0.13

*NB kcal per weight values will vary according to cooking or if raw. The following values are based on lightly cooked.

Conclusion

Please share your opinion on Amazon

We hope you are enjoying making these recipes for your precious puppy. We would really love to hear which are your favorites. If you have any suggestions or requests, please also tell us about them so that we can improve future editions to benefit other like-minded owners. I really appreciate any help you can provide.

Please submit your review on Amazon

Printed in Great Britain
by Amazon

49816636R00137